# THINNING
# BLOOD

# THINNING
# BLOOD

A MEMOIR OF FAMILY, MYTH,
AND IDENTITY

LEAH MYERS

W. W. NORTON & COMPANY
*Celebrating a Century of Independent Publishing*

Some of the pieces in this book appeared in slightly different form in the following publications: "The Sound of the End" in *Fugue* (Fall 2021); "A Writer Who Can't Read" in *Yellow Arrow Journal* (May 2021); "A Letter to My Seventh-Generation Descendant" in *CRAFT* (April 2021); and "Skinwalker" in *Gasher* (Fall 2020). The author is grateful to the editors of these publications.

For information about special discounts for bulk purchases, please contact W. W. Norton Special Sales at specialsales@wwnorton.com or 800-233-4830

Manufacturing by Lake Book Manufacturing
Book design by Chris Welch
Production manager: Anna Oler

ISBN 978-1-324-03670-8

W. W. Norton & Company, Inc.
500 Fifth Avenue, New York, N.Y. 10110
www.wwnorton.com

W. W. Norton & Company Ltd.
15 Carlisle Street, London W1D 3BS

1 2 3 4 5 6 7 8 9 0

*To my family, who listen to me even when my
words are harsh.*

*To Connor, Téo, and Kirsten, for listening to me rant and
ramble as this book came to life.*

*And to Blane, for supporting me, loving me, and making me
feel like I can do anything.*

# Contents

# THINNING
# BLOOD

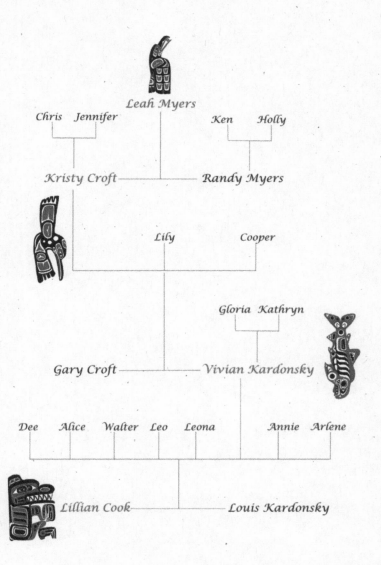

# INTRODUCTION:

## A LINEAGE

No one taught me to be Native American. My mother taught me that I was, but she did not have the context for what that heritage meant. My grandmother mentioned it very little, even though it was visible in her features. Yet from my earliest memories, being Native has always been an integral part of my identity. Even though I was raised far from my tribe, far from any tribe, I heard the drumbeat of our traditions in my heart. My name is Leah Kallen Myers. I am the last member of the Jamestown S'Klallam Tribe in my family line.

My family has always called me the record keeper. I collect the stories of those who came before me, of all my family members. I have suitcases and shoeboxes full of photos, and notebooks full of stories. I aim to make memories tangible, physical, so they are harder to forget.

In being the record keeper, I must construct parts of history from fragments. To my knowledge, I am the only woman in this lineage who has connected with her totem, also called one's Spirit Animal, on her own. Mine is Raven. No one knew my great-grandmother Lillian's animal, but after hearing stories of her strength and protective nature, it is clear to me that she was Bear. Vivian, my granny, was raised to think our stories make us look foolish and simple. Even though she reconnected with the traditions later in life, some self-loathing was too deep-rooted to let go. She was in a constant swim upriver, fighting against the world around her. She was Salmon, the symbol of sacrifice and determination. Kristy, my mom, never had the opportunity to think of her own connection to our culture. We have discussed Spirit Animals often, and I suggested Hummingbird, the symbol of spirituality, love, and joy. It clicked in her soul. I have learned and modified the legends for each of these Spirits, and tell them so that they reflect the women of my life even more. My family history is shrouded enough, lost enough, that it is myth itself and blends easily with the legends of my people to create a seamless new record for the world.

I don't want other Native Americans to go without, like my family has for so long. I want to give my generation a voice. I was born to tell my story and the story of my people, to make everyone aware that we exist still, that we breathe still.

Totem poles are used to represent stories, or places, and in my case, the totem pole I have created in my mind represents my family. I picture this carved monument standing alone in a clearing within the Washington rainforest. Its painted faces, though worn in places, show Bear, Salmon, Hummingbird, and, perched at the top, Raven. I am here to carve that same totem pole into the minds of others, so we will not be forgotten when we are gone.

The phrase "low man on the totem pole" was coined by a White man in the 1940s to mean a person with no respect, status, or power. He clearly did not consult the Natives who carve the poles. They honor the figures they represent by immortalizing them in precious old-growth red cedar. Each member of the totem pole is significant, but the one on the bottom is often given the most reverence. They are the one who holds up everyone else; they are the one who starts the story.

There is no space left at the top of my totem pole lineage for the next generation. Even if I do have children, they will only be one-sixteenth S'Klallam. This is not enough tribal blood to carry the title of tribal member according to our blood quantum laws.

Blood quantum refers to the percentage of blood an individual must have to be considered Native American; every tribal nation has a different requirement. Laws regulating these amounts started as a colonizer practice to erase the Native people by limiting tribal citizenship but have since been adopted by some tribes in an attempt to preserve their culture. When my tribe was first federally recognized, the requirement set by the US government was one-fourth S'Klallam blood in your veins. In 1994, a year after I was born, the Tribal Council codified a new set of requirements: one-eighth blood and the ability to trace your ancestry back to a full-blooded tribal member.

No matter how my family tree may grow, the tribal citizenship stops with me. This is why my role as storyteller means more than ever; I will not see my culture turn into smoke blown away by the winds of time. So much has been lost already.

The Creator brought the S'Klallam people from the Elwha River on the Olympic Peninsula in what would come to be known as Washington State. The people were bathed in the waters of the river as they emerged from rocks shaped like coiled baskets. These rocks held the life force of the land and water, and still sit lodged in the river's bank today.

The people emerged from the waters and went into a forest. The area around them was lush and green, with trees that attempted to touch the sky and catch clouds in their branches. To the north was the Salish Sea, a deep body of water whose tides rose and fell like the newly found breath in their chests. To the south were the mountains, ancient hands of the earth that shielded the coastline from what may lay beyond. All around the S'Klallam people were animals, creatures who watched them with curious eyes. These creatures would come to take part in their later stories and help carve the world further into what it was always meant to be.

The S'Klallam would go on to be nomadic, moving from place to place along the coastline with the seasons. They were fishers, hunters, and crafters, taking just enough from the world around them to thrive and grow. They carved canoes from red cedar so they could journey out onto the sea. They traversed the mountains and learned the land that they called home. They wove baskets that resembled the coiling shape of the rocks from which they were born and told the story of their creation to their children. For generations to come the S'Klallam people told the story of the Creator and the ways they shaped the world.

At some point, they stopped. The rocks were drowned; the

river was dammed. When the stone coils were rediscovered years later, the story of the S'Klallam emergence had been reduced to two lines. *The Elwha River has two large rocks called coiled baskets. It is there that the Creator bathed and blessed the people.*

They had forgotten. We had forgotten.

Now I must imagine and put it back together as best I can.

I am Lillian's great-granddaughter and I have her strength.

I am Vivian's granddaughter and I have her determination.

I am Kristy's daughter and I have her compassion.

I am Leah, and I have my voice and a story to tell.

# I

# Bear

*The bear is a symbol of motherly love and familial strength in the fiercest way. A mother bear will not allow her children to come to harm, but she will not coddle them either. No one dares come between the mother and her cubs, but still her cubs must keep up with her and learn to be strong themselves.*

The clearing where my imagined totem pole stands becomes shrouded in fog when I think of Bear. Her carved edges at the base of the pole have rounded with time and weather. It is cracked, and much of the paint has chipped or faded. This is a part of my history that exists only in watered-down legends. It is a time of perseverance and survival in a period of erasure.

# A LEGEND OF THE
## BEAR MOTHER

I t all starts with berries.

The women of the Coast Salish tribes are supposed to just pick berries and return home, and never cause a fuss. One woman has too much fire in her. While they are out, she steps in bear dung. Quiet is not the way of this woman. She curses and spits vitriol. She can't accept her fault and instead blames the bears. She calls them unclean, weaves insults against the whole bear tribe into her tirade.

Fate puts two bears within earshot.

Bears are proud creatures. They stand their ground when challenged and defend their homes and their dignity. They stand to this challenge too. The more powerful of the two transforms himself into a man, one more handsome and striking than you can imagine. He approaches the fiery woman, cutting her shouts short.

There is no record of what is said, but he charms her. A blinding smile will only get you so far. Something about him connects with her.

He asks her to come back to his mountain home. She agrees.

Here is where we expect the legend to become a tragedy, or a lesson. We expect the woman to be tortured or raped or held prisoner. It would serve as a lesson to always be kind or to be mindful of yourself or to just keep your mouth shut if you are a woman.

But that isn't how the legend goes.

She arrives at his home, Bear Village, high in the peaks of the mountains. Whatever spark made her agree to come solidifies into love. And he, somewhere along the journey, falls in love with her too. Maybe he doesn't realize it until she's at his home and it seems like she was always meant to be there. Maybe it isn't until he realizes how boring his life would seem without this newfound fire in it. It doesn't matter; he loves her.

Bear Village welcomes her. They help her set up her home and do not raise too many questions at the unusual couple the two make, being from such different worlds. The woman is still a human but chooses to look and act like a bear as much as she can, because the bear tribe has accepted her. She marries the bear who brought her home and they have many children. The children are even more talented at transforming than their father; they seamlessly move between forms. If fate were always kind, they would know how strong they are and bring peace and harmony between the human and bear tribes once and for all.

Instead, fate brings the woman's family to Bear Village. Her brothers refuse to accept that she would leave her tribe for the beasts willingly. They believe at first that she is a prisoner, then decide she must just be crazy.

In some versions of this story, the brothers walk away. They disown the woman, and she learns to make her way through the world with her love by her side. It is difficult, but she is strong and her spirit burns bright.

Fate is not so generous in the original legend.

The brothers refuse to leave without the woman and her children. They challenge the bear who brought her to his home to a contest, but they don't fight fair. They overpower and kill the bear.

The woman breaks. Her brothers drag her back to their coastal village while she kicks and screams. She probably tries to kill them herself because she is fire and grief is fuel. She and her children are brought back to the tribe's village but are never fully accepted by the community. She dies, likely of a broken heart, or maybe they kill her to douse the burning rage for good.

The woman's children belong nowhere. They are uncomfortable around their mother's tribe; they never bathed in that culture. They cannot return home for fear of violent revenge by Bear Village for the death of their father. They carry the guilt of their parents' deaths with them into the woods, forging a new path that will be forever between the bears of the mountain and the shores of humankind.

# REAL LIVE INDIANS

G abby transferred to my school in the fourth grade. She had blonde hair and blue eyes and was tanner than most of the other White girls in my class for no apparent reason. In one of my clearer memories of her, her face is snarled and in a shrill, whiny voice she is saying to me, "Stop lying, you're not an Indian!"

Nine-year-old me didn't have many years of experience with racism. This was the first time someone had even questioned the validity of my ethnicity, let alone outright called me a liar. Back then, I didn't have the ability or knowledge to point to the media representation of Native Americans to show Gabby how she had been taught to think that my culture was gone. At nine years old I lacked the words to explain that her ignorance did not and would never define who I was. Those tools simply hadn't been given to me yet.

So I punched her in the face.

≫

In 1907, the photographer Edward S. Curtis started a twenty-volume series of heavily illustrated books titled *The North American Indian*. The first photo in the first volume is titled "The Vanishing Race." It depicted a group of Navajo riding horses on a classic western trail, with dust and brush that gave way to mesas in the distance. He wanted to capture the picturesque Indian life before it disappeared forever. His work would later go on to be dramatized by Marie Clements, exemplifying the way that good intentions can lead to disastrous outcomes and disappointment for the artist and their subject both.

Curtis took his photographs to try to show Native Americans as a "noble" race, but unfortunately all he did was pave the road to hell. Not hell for Curtis though, just for the people he was trying to preserve. His depiction of a culture—seen through the White lens as endangered and other—cemented the stereotype that Native Americans were dying out. Of course, good capitalists never miss an opportunity. Soon after the publications started, railroad companies sniffed out a profit and began advertising to tourists the chance to see the last of a dying people. Native Americans became seen as obsolete and anachronistic, a people that didn't belong in modern society.

To this day there are constant battles with individuals and corporations to try and make people understand that we aren't going anywhere. In July 2015, representatives of Chevron were denied access to Unist'ot'en land to do a survey as the first step in building a new pipeline. The Unist'ot'en are a Native tribe in Northern British Columbia. Under a 2014 decision by the Supreme Court of Canada, anyone who wanted to engage in activity on tribal land had to engage in meaningful consultation with the tribe before they could proceed. Presumably as part of, or instead of, an effort to engage in "meaningful consultation," three Chevron representatives actually offered representatives of the Unist'ot'en tribe a case of water and two cartons of cigarettes. They spoke as if those items were a generous peace offering. They thought of these living, breathing people as antiques. They believed that appearing with cheap offerings would be enough to persuade the tribe to let them go forward with their pipeline.

As a Native American, I appreciate the sentiment Curtis carried, but all he did was put water on a grease fire.

➤

The first time I set foot in my tribal homelands, I was twelve years old. We traveled to Washington from my home state of Georgia, where my grandparents had moved when my grandfather retired. Only one memory has crystallized from that trip, a moment in time that I can go back to and feel every second pass.

The Olympic Peninsula is covered in lush forests that blanket mountains. The pines stretch high into the sky, and looking out to the horizon from a mountain crest feels like looking into a painting. The mountains are often snowcapped, and their blue silhouettes against the lighter sky is a calming sight for me. This calming sensation has been with me since the very beginning: everything there felt familiar the first time I encountered it, like I had always known the land.

My parents and I were hiking Hurricane Ridge, not far from where the family reunion was held. The trails lead into mountains and around several crests and clearings in the old-growth rain-forest that shows the area's age.

After our hike we went to the visitor center, which sat on a rounded patch free of trees that overlooked the forest below and made one eye level with another mountain ridge in the distance. I sat to take in the view. The wind blew just hard enough to push my heavy, unkempt hair back. I filled my lungs with the cool air and felt roots begin to take hold. I had always been a restless person, even at this early point in life, and this was a new experience: peace. I felt as though the trees and earth of the mountain reached up into my soul and curled around it, making it whole. The inky blackness I had yet to name, the dark pit that buzzed just below my surface and corroded my thoughts, was quieted. For a moment, it was like I didn't feel it at all.

When my mom asked me what was wrong, I told her exactly how I felt as best I could.

"My home is in Georgia, but my soul is at home here."

꙳

Up to 95 percent of the original Native American population, estimated at roughly twenty million people, disappeared after the invasion of European colonizers. While there was direct violence toward Native Americans, many of these deaths can be attributed to the introduction of smallpox. Smallpox is a virus that is spread when one comes into contact with infected bodily fluids or contaminated objects such as clothing or blankets. The virus then finds its way into a person's lymphatic system. Within days of infection, large, painful pustules begin to erupt over the victim's skin.

In school curriculums, this has often been taught as an unfortunate tragedy, an accidental side effect of trade, and therefore a reason to claim that the Europeans did not commit genocide. However, in recent years, many historians have recognized that the spreading of smallpox was an early form of biological warfare, one which was understood and used without mercy from at least the mid-1700s. Noted conversations among army officials include letters discussing the idea of "sending the Small Pox among those disaffected tribes" and using "every stratagem to reduce them." Another official, Henry Bouquet, wrote a letter that told his subordinates to "try to Innoculate [sic] the Indians, by means of Blankets, as well as to Try Every other Method, that can serve to Extirpate this Execrable Race." They followed through on their plan, giving two blankets and a handkerchief from the Smallpox Hospital alongside other gifts to seal an agreement of friendship between the local Native tribes and the men at Fort Pitt, located in what is now western Pennsylvania.

This, and other similar efforts like it across the country, destroyed the Native American population, which led to Curtis's and others belief that they would soon "disappear." The modern Native American population is growing from its rock bottom numbers, reaching around 9.7 million as of the 2020 census. However, even with those numbers, we still remain only 2.9 percent of the population of the nation that tried so hard to eliminate us. No one wanted to use the word *murder* then, using instead words more apt to talking about a pest problem than a human race. Even today the United States still has not officially recognized genocide in its history.

No one wanted to take back the blankets either.

≫•

In 2013, when I was living in Arizona and attending college, I went on a spring break vacation to Albuquerque, New Mexico, with my friend Miranda. Miranda was very pale, with bright blue eyes and thin, manageable hair. We were sitting at the continental breakfast of the Best Western we were calling home that week. Miranda was a morning person and therefore was chatting with a family, a middle-aged woman with her kids and her mother. I am not and have never been a morning person, so I was trying very hard to ignore the conversation and eat my lackluster bacon and bagel. However, the woman was very loud. They were from the UK. They were touring the US.

"We're on our way to the Grand Canyon!" the woman said. She used big gestures and smiled too wide in her "I Heart Albuquerque" tank top. She was clearly a morning person.

"Oh, that's cool!" Miranda said, equally as cheery. "We're from Arizona. You're going to love it; it's beautiful there."

"That's what we've heard!" She leaned down, pressing both of her hands into the table. "And we paid for the tour into the Canyon. We're going to go down into it and see real, live Indians!"

Miranda immediately began to laugh. She bent over her plate

of muffins, body shaking and eyes squeezed shut. The woman's face was blank, then slowly morphed into offended confusion. Her hands were still pressed into the table, and she turned her full attention toward me; now her posture looked more like a cop conducting an interrogation. She said nothing but her face shouted, *What's so funny?*

"She's laughing because I'm actually Native American," I said. I resisted the urge to do jazz hands at this woman, and instead offered up whatever a fake smile looks like at too-damn-early in the morning.

This stranger took a moment to regard me. I wondered how the cogs were turning in her head as she looked me over. Her mind must have been full of images of the Noble Savage, a warrior in a headdress standing tall on a cliff or a hill and letting out a hand-over-mouth war cry. Instead, her first interaction with a real, live Indian was a grouchy twenty-something girl, in an oversized Fall Out Boy T-shirt in the forgettable breakfast parlor of an equally forgettable Best Western.

Her stare felt like it lasted at least twenty years, but finally she spoke. "Oh," she said, returning to a normal standing posture and gesturing at me with an open palm and a half-shrug. "Well, congratulations! Good for you!"

Miranda, who had just recovered from her previous fit of laughter, broke into hysterics again.

"Um," was all I managed to get out at first. I wanted to devour this woman's dignity. Congratulations for what exactly? For having a family who made it through genocide? For being part of the slim population of surviving Native Americans post-colonization? An anger simmered in my throat, begging to be let loose on this stupid woman who was there to simply enjoy her vacation. How dare she remain blissfully unaware of the modern existence of Native Americans when all she had seen were movies making us look like history? As mad as I was, I knew it wasn't just her fault and I couldn't muster up the energy to boil my anger into a response.

"Thank you?" I asked.

She did not take it as a question. "You're welcome," she said in her still too-bright voice. She excused herself to go get more food shortly after, and I threw out my breakfast, having lost my appetite.

Later that day Miranda and I went to the Petroglyph National Monument. There were hundreds of carvings in volcanic rocks of men and masks and armadillos. The pamphlet we were given talked about how the park was in place to protect an ancient culture. The pamphlet never mentioned the Navajo reservation down the road.

⇝

Indian boarding schools began in 1860, with the first school being established on the Yakima Indian Reservation in Washington State. These schools were designed to take Native American youths and mold them into members of "civilized society"; to make them White. The schools taught the basics of education, such as arithmetic, but also taught the students to practice Christianity and that the political structures of the United States were ideal for everyone. The actual goal was to eradicate every ounce of Native cultures.

By the 1880s, it was decided that boarding schools on the reservation were not removed enough from the Native American way of life. They couldn't kill the students' spirit and cultural connection fully while on their homeland. To assimilationists, whose goal it was to erase our existence, off-reservation boarding schools were the best way to bring Native children into the folds of White society.

Here enters Colonel Richard Henry Pratt, a man on every modern Native American's shit list. Pratt created the Carlisle Indian Industrial School in Carlisle, Pennsylvania, and his motto was "kill the Indian, save the man." At this school, and others that would open and follow in its wake, tens of thousands of Native children faced abuse and neglect. They were often forcibly removed from their homes and taken to these schools that were sometimes across the country from their original lives. When they arrived, the children were forced to cut their hair and change their names. They were made to become White in look and label, stripped of any semblance of Native heritage. The children were not allowed to speak their Native tongues, some of them not knowing anything else. They were prohibited from acting in any way that might reflect the only culture they had ever known.

At Pratt's Carlisle Indian Industrial School alone, the numbers revealed the truth of what this treatment did. Of the ten thousand children from 141 different tribes across the country, only a small fraction of them ever graduated. According to the Carlisle Indian School Project, there are 180 marked graves of Native children who died while attending. There were even more children who died while held captive at the Carlisle school and others across the country. Their bodies are only being discovered in modern times, exhumed by the army and people doing surveys of the land who are finding unmarked burial sites. An autograph book from one of the schools was found in the historical records with one child's message to a friend, "Please remember me when I'm in the grave."

The US Bureau of Indian Affairs seemed to think Pratt had the right idea and made his school the model for more. There ended up being more than 350 government-funded boarding schools for Natives in the United States. Most of them followed the same ideology: Never let the children be themselves. Beat their language out of them. Punish them for practicing their cultures.

Pratt and his followers certainly killed plenty of Indians, but they didn't save a damn thing.

➤

On St. Patrick's Day 2015, I was drinking with my White then husband and two friends, Mary and Ken. We were roughly three Guinness–whiskey shot combos deep when Ken started talking statistics. For reference, he was from a certain kind of White family, the ones with loud ideas about patriotism and America that are passed down from generation to generation. They were the kind to claim they bleed red, white, and blue.

"You know," his voice was confident, even as he slurred, "in like twenty years, we are going to be the minority." He was looking at each of us in turn, trying to make sure we understood.

I didn't understand. "What do you mean, we?"

"You know," he gestured broadly to all four of us sitting in the room, "White people."

My face betrayed how confused I was, and how quickly that confusion was morphing into indignant anger. Even drunk I tried to use what logic I had left to bite my tongue and let it go.

"That's so fucking scary," Mary said. She leaned back and looked at the ceiling, her bleached blonde hair spread out like a fan on the sofa behind her. "Like, that's really terrifying."

I looked to my husband for some sort of backup on how insane this all was, but he was too deep into the liquor to even register that a conversation was happening. He was curled over a pillow, rocking slowly with his eyes half closed.

I addressed Mary first. "Why is it scary?" I had never seen this side of either of them, even when drunk.

"Well, I mean, think about it, Leah." She sat back up and leaned in, unblinking and serious. "We've all been treating minorities like shit for years. They're probably going to like, kill us or something."

I couldn't take the use of "we" anymore, especially in this context. "You guys know I'm not White . . . right?"

Mary and Ken both looked at me, not apologetic—just confused. "Of course, you're White," Ken finally said.

"No, I'm not, I'm Native American." I felt the blade edge in my voice and did my very best to remind myself how drunk they both were. Clearly now they would understand and apologize, and we would move on.

Mary laughed. It was a loud, relieved laugh. "Oh well, yeah, everybody is some part Indian!" She saw the look on my face and pushed my shoulder in an attempt at camaraderie. "You're basically White; it's fine." She went into the kitchen to fix herself another drink.

Ken visibly relaxed in his seat. "I was so worried you were going to say you were part Mexican or something."

As I was trying to decide how to end both of the friendships on the spot without screaming, like I truly wanted to, my very drunk husband vomited on their floor, and rug, and couch, and pillow that he had been cuddling. It smelled like Guinness, curdled Baileys, and bile. Between cleaning up puke and them letting us stay the night, I lost the chance to say anything. Through hungover breakfast, Mary and Ken were as friendly as ever. I didn't have many friends, so I took their hatred in stride. But I made it a point to speak out against any mockeries of Native American culture when we were together, and any other racial stereotypes as well. It wasn't much, but over time it made them both uncomfortable enough to quietly leave my life.

≈

I moved to Sequim, Washington, the home of my tribe, in 2017, once I had graduated college. I needed to get away from the desert of Arizona that I had called home for nearly ten years. As I drove toward my new home, I went through Blyn, a blip of a town—the start of the one thousand acres that my tribe owns. When I made it around the first curve on Highway 101, I saw the tribal center. The buildings, one to the east on a hill and one to the west on the beach of Sequim Bay, were cream colored with green roofs. There were tall, vibrant totem poles carved from nine-hundred-year-old cedar to represent both our founding fathers and stories and lore. The bus station had carvings of our histories and legends. The fire station, which my tribe paid for so that the entire town of Blyn would have first responders, bears symbols of protection on its walls. Everywhere my culture is thriving; my people are thriving.

I called my mom and told her I had made it. We talked about when I'd visited as a child, and how it had all felt to me then, welcome and familiar even though I had spent little time here. We talked about the connection I made on the mountain top.

Driving along this coast in this tiny town, I felt it again: the roots reaching into me to take hold of my soul. After years of friends and strangers trying to erase my history, I was surrounded by the physical proof of our existence. Every totem pole and carving, done by the hands of my fellow tribal members, stood as a testament to years of a people thriving. The land I drove on and walked on was ours. I was breathing the air that every previous generation had breathed. I was passing by the bay and rivers they fished in and through the forests we have always called home. I was in the beating heart of the land that my stories and legends emerged from. I could finally rest assured again.

We are here and alive.

# AN ANNOTATED GUIDE TO
## ANTI-NATIVE SLURS

*Apple*—A Native American who is red on the outside, but White on the inside. The term *apple* can be used by either Whites or Natives, though it is more commonly used by Natives in reference to other Natives. It comes from the visual appearance of the fruit and is thought to originate during the 1980s.

When I learned this slur it stuck like a thorn. I felt like it was carved from malice especially for me. I've never been able to shake that feeling.

*Also: Radish.*

*Chug*—A name in reference to the "Drunken Indian" stereotype. This stereotype dates back to at least the late 1700s, when a Catholic priest described the Ottawa people as "passionately attached" to brandy. This myth has since appeared widely in movies, TV shows, books, and other forms of media. The assumption of addiction has also spread from alcohol to huffing gas. Of course, painting a people in a negative light is the best way to get away with treating them poorly.

Learning this term stung a little less because I knew about the stereotype already. I often try not to think of the long list of family members who struggle with addiction in this context. I'm not ashamed, but sometimes I feel like I should be.

*Also: Blackout, Gas Huffer, Gasbag, Huff.*

*Cochise*—Any Native American, though more commonly used for those who are outspoken or who stand their ground. This is a reference to the Chiricahua Apache chief, Cochise, who was made famous during the 1860s and 1870s for his resistance to White colonizers during the Apache Wars. Sometimes meant as a compliment, but it isn't. Uncertain origin date as a slur.

I hear this slur in movies where the person saying this word is supposed to be a hero. At an old job, I heard my boss call people chief all the time. One time he said, "Too many chiefs, not enough Indians" and when I confronted him, he didn't remember saying it at all.

*Also: Geronimo, Chief.*

*Gut-Eater*—Refers to the Native American belief that no part of the animal should be wasted. Colonizers believed that eating stomach lining was beneath them, and therefore considered this an insult. During the invasion of the West, Whites massacred buffalo and left behind only the intestines and stomach, forcing Plains tribes to subsist off guts alone.

This ignorant reference makes me want to remind anyone who uses it how their ancestors likely would have starved without mine.

*Also: Maize-muncher, Salmon-cruncher, Seal-clubber.*

*Indian*—Common enough to not be immediately recognized as a slur, it is sometimes the preferred term of identification by a Native American. This term originates from the invader Christopher Columbus, who believed at first that he had reached India. Unable to admit his mistake originally, he dubbed the Taíno people whom he met as "Indians." The name has stuck ever since. Originated 1493.

It doesn't matter how many times I hear it, I will always cringe a little and find myself unable to hide the anger that flares on my face whenever a non-Native says this word.

*Also: Injun, Eskimo.*

*Pretendian*—A person who claims to be Native but isn't, according to the person using the term. This is used often among Natives in reference to people who claim Native heritage when they are not Native, especially in circumstances such as applying for limited scholarships or college admission. It can also reference individuals with lower blood quantum, who some believe should not be able to claim Native American heritage.

I don't label myself with this because I know who I am and where I came from. Yet I do wonder how often people call me this behind my back.

*Also: Box Checker.*

*Redskin*—Commonly believed to be used because of the red tone of Native skin. While this may have been the original source for the first uses of the term, starting as early as 1769 and into the early 1800s, it is not necessarily the most widespread use. One common application of the term was in the practice of scalp hunting. In 1863, a Minnesota newspaper called *The Daily Republican* printed the following announcement: "The state reward for dead Indians has been increased to $200 for every red-skin sent to Purgatory. This sum is more than the dead bodies of all the Indians east of the Red River are worth."

This is one slur that makes me want to snarl and fight whenever I hear it. It's vile that it was the name of a professional football team for so long. I always point out how other countries censor its use on TV. People usually call me too sensitive and that just makes me want to fight even more.

*Savage*—Ascribes an inherently uncivilized or violent nature to Native Americans. This term was used originally to describe the nature of wild beasts, implying that the people indigenous to the land that Europeans colonized were less than human. The word evokes a mercilessness and lack of complex thought in the people it is meant to describe, despite evidence to the contrary.

I first encountered this as a child while watching *Pocahontas*. Even though no one had taught me what it meant, I never felt comfortable singing that part of the song "Savages (Part I)," the part where White people wished death on my whole race, but I sang it anyway.

Also: *Cowboy Killer, Knee Jerk, Hatchet Packer, Scalper, Siwash, Tomahawk Chucker, Wagon Burner.*

*Squaw*—A female Native American. This word has origins in Algonquian, where the word does refer to the totality of being female. However, since colonizers began writing about the tribes they encountered, the word *squaw* began to connote a sexual or derogatory meaning. One early example of this is from the 1892 novel *An Algonquin Maiden*, in which the heroine being called a squaw is "a glaring accusation against her virtue."

My first interaction with this word was also as a child, during the movie *Peter Pan*. The caricature of a Native woman calls Wendy, who is White, a squaw but does not use the same word for Tiger Lily, who is Native. Now I know that she thought Wendy was a slut; but the little revelation that the Native woman was held in higher regard for once still doesn't outweigh my disgust at the song "What Makes the Red Man Red" that is sung during the same scene.

*Also: Buck, Squaw Hopper.*

*Tonto*—Native American character on *The Lone Ranger* TV show. This is the epitome of the "Noble Savage" stereotype; a Native, often male, who will help the White man in all of his endeavors. The word is also Spanish for "stupid," which is how the targets of this term are often perceived by the people who use it.

When I hear this slur, I think of Sherman Alexie's book of stories, *The Lone Ranger and Tonto Fistfight in Heaven*. It was my introduction into Native literature, and I've known my path ever since. At the time, Alexie was the most prominent Native voice I had encountered. The influence of his work stayed with me for a long time. Before the sexual harassment allegations that later came to light, his writing—his existence as a Native author writing about Native experiences—led me to seek more, learn more. I craved hearing voices like mine. I found Joy Harjo, an author of memoirs and a United States Poet Laureate for three terms. And I discovered Natalie Diaz, whose collection of poetry, *When My Brother Was an Aztec*, I memorized from reading it over and over. When she visited Arizona State University, I had the opportunity to watch her read and speak, and I talked with her briefly. I was awestruck and empowered that day. I wasn't as shy to tell my own stories anymore because I knew I wasn't alone.

# BEAR'S DECISION

Even colonizers have applied the idiom "Mama Bear" when talking about a mother violently defending her children. In Native cultures, bears are a symbol of strength and protection too. They stand their ground, even when challenged. Nearly everyone, regardless of skin tone, knows you don't come between a bear and her cubs.

That's why it's so shocking that bears sometimes eat their young.

≫•

My great-grandmother, Lillian Cook Kardonsky, was the last full-blooded member of the Jamestown S'Klallam Tribe in her family line. She fell in love with a quiet, kind, Russian Jewish immigrant named Louis Kardonsky. He was running from a past and a family whom he never spoke of. Rumors flew about where he was from: a moonshiner's son running from the shady goings on, or an illegal immigrant fleeing Russia's tightening grasp. He feared the US government and being deported back to his home country. I have seen the way the women of my family fall in love, and I can almost guarantee Lillian never thought twice about any of that.

I imagine that they met on the beach. They both would have spent a lot of time there, as neither drove and there weren't many other places to go. I think that Louis would have been relaxing, watching the water, and then heard some screams in a language he didn't speak. They would have sounded like curses, just from the vitriol behind them. He, being a kind soul who generally wants to help, would have walked toward the yelling. He would come across a Native woman with a tangled fishing net: Lillian. He would have let a small chuckle escape, because the image of a woman screaming at a net is absurd. She would have turned on him, ready to start her next round of curses. Before she would have the chance to do so, he would hold his hands up defensively, and ask if he can help. His words would be sincere and gentle, and she would have been able to tell so instantly. She would have reluctantly agreed, and they would spend some time untangling the net as the sun got lower in the sky. He would have offered to help her fish, or make her dinner, or even just walk along the beach with her until nightfall. She would have found him charming and calming. They would have been almost in love before the evening was done.

Of course, that's only in my mind. No one knows the real story of how they met. It's another record lost to time. We only know that they met, fell in love, and married despite the consequences.

Their marriage was a scandal among the tribal members. Her own mother, Nora Cook, whom Lillian took in and cared for when her own children were still young, despised the young family. Nora was immobile, and all eight of Lillian's children took turns helping carry the small woman to and from the bathroom and brought meals to her. She never uttered a thank you, but instead called them the Klallam slang for crazy White men. When Nora's full-blooded Native grandchildren were around, she doted on them. She called them each "sweet child" in her native tongue in front of the children she admonished for existing. Lillian cared for her mother until the end in spite of that. My family never speaks about it, but I am sure Lillian was furious that her children were spoken to in such a way and treated so unfairly, with only her respect for her elders outweighing her rage.

⋙•

Bears eat their young when times are hard.

Or when the cubs aren't quite right.

Or if the cub dies, to make sure the scent of rot doesn't spread.

I know plenty of mammal mothers that exhibit this behavior, but I don't care about the others. Bears are supposed to protect their young. They are the symbol of motherly love and guardianship. They should be better, but sometimes aren't.

⋙•

Lillian and Louis and their children were treated poorly by the general White community in the area because they were still Indians and immigrants. The only support they had were each other and the White Pentecostal church they attended. White churches at the time were still largely subscribing to the notion of "kill the Indian, save the man," making them more welcoming to the Native people than the general community, so long as the Natives were willing to let go of their traditional beliefs. Her children were taught to present and speak as White as possible. They were never taught their ancestral language or taken to participate in cultural events. Lillian sought to shield them from the world who hated their "savage" hearts, and in doing so severed the connection to that heart entirely.

Sometimes, I want to ask these mother bears why they are sometimes so cruel. I want to scream and shout at them, to make them realize what darkness they have created. I have a myriad of questions to ask them.

*Don't you see how much they love you?*

*Don't you see how they need your guidance? How they need a shield?*

*Can't you see that they are vulnerable because you made them that way?*

*How can you not see that they are still part of you, still strong?*

*How could you give up on them?*

*Don't you know your actions end your line? If you destroy them, what will be left of you?*

I can guess at the answers.

*Love is less important than preservation.*

*I did guide them the best I could, for as long as I could.*

*They weren't strong enough to weather what was coming.*

*I only gave up on part of them.*

*My line in the future is less important than the world before me now.*

⇝

In the face of difficulty, Lillian ran her home tight and lean. She was determined to rise above the stigma of the "Dirty, Lazy Indian" stereotype. The floor was swept after every meal, no matter the number of crumbs. Each Saturday the entire family pulled every piece of furniture they owned out of the home. The house was cleaned by hand, with every family member doing their part, from the youngest child to Lillian and Louis themselves. Items were slowly returned to their proper places over the course of the day; rugs and couches settling in until the same time next week. Even with this demanding cleaning schedule Lillian found the time to make her children's clothes and cook their meals. She managed her diabetes while handling eleven children over the years, three of whom were not her own but nephews and a niece she took in after her estranged sister passed away.

The entire family was piled into a small home on Sequim beach, which at the time was considered to be the poor immigrant area. They had no electricity or plumbing and relied on the kids fetching water for cooking. Despite the humble nature of these beginnings, she taught her children to be strong and proud.

She may not have taught them to be proud to be Native, but she did teach them to be proud.

∽•

I never wanted to hate my Bear, Lillian. For a long time, I looked up to her and the wild love story she had. She found someone so unlike her that fit her completely. She was explosive, loud, firm in her stance. He was gentle and soft, humming to himself instead of yelling at others whenever he got upset. She shunned her world for the world they would build together.

Then I realized her actions were part of what led to the end. Her desire to scrub the red from the skin of her children led to our culture being bleached out. Her actions also led to me, perched at the top of my familial totem pole with nowhere to go. Her carving still stands strong at the bottom of that totem pole, set in its decision. The cracks on its surface that I cannot fill seem now to be made not by time, but by bear claws.

I wouldn't be here without my Bear's choices: her decision to marry outside of her race or to raise her children against their heritage. Still, different choices—like marrying another tribal citizen or teaching her children that Natives are not inherently dirty and lesser than—may have led to a tribe with stronger numbers, one that was flourishing and growing and expanding in numbers instead of slowly dying out. One that was not filled with finished totem pole lineages that dot the wide expanse of a land we've come to claim.

When that feathered darkness under the surface of my soul rises up and wraps around my heart and mind, I wonder if she would still think it was all worth it. If I'm worth that sacrifice.

# II

# Salmon

*The salmon is a symbol of prosperity and determination to the Coast Salish tribes, the band of tribes in the Pacific Northwest of which the Jamestown S'Klallam Tribe is a part. She defies nature, swimming upstream to provide for the people of the land. Yet she must sacrifice herself to give that abundance to others. Her determination comes at a deep personal cost.*

Salmon on the totem pole in my mind has been altered. Her nature is visible, but the original colors have been faded by more than just the hands of time; the vibrant red that Salmon started with was removed, severed by a mother's love and societal rejection. When the story of Salmon is told the air is colder. It is a time to remember what has been lost on the path to prosperity. It is a time to acknowledge that some people live between two worlds, the same way that Salmon lives between the river and the sea.

# A LEGEND OF SALMON WOMAN

T he Salish people were starving.

In the original legend, they call to male spirits for help. In my version we will cut out the middleman.

Salmon Woman sees the people starving from her ocean home. She has many children, all surrounding her. She loves her children, but she loves the people too. She wants to reach out to them, to help them, to have someone outside of her family accept her.

A deal is struck. The Salish people can fish some of her children. They can catch them and kill them and eat them. Salmon Woman believes she will get to keep most of her children safe and happy, living year-round in the mouth of the river. She will be

adored and loved and cherished for her sacrifice. Her children are
not given a choice as to which world they will live in or whether
their lives are worth more or less than those of the Salish people.

Time passes; people forget. They forget the ferocity of a hunger
that feels like it is eating your insides to quell its own starvation.
They call the Salmon Woman lovely and tell her she's the prettiest
salmon they've ever seen while they cull her children from the river's mouth. At first, she basks in the compliments, the belonging.
Eventually she realizes that her children are dwindling, and she
is left with just seven, one for each species of salmon: Pink, Sockeye, Coho, Chum, Chinook, Cutthroat, and Steelhead. Her fear
overrides her vanity. She collects her children in the night and
flees to her father's home beneath the ocean waves. She promises
her children they would never return to the river; that she would
never endanger them again.

Starvation creeps back into the coastal village. It thins their
bodies and dwindles their spirits. Salmon Woman watches from
the safety of the sea. Guilt eats away at her. She made a promise.
People are dying because of her. Her children will die if she fol-
lows through on her promises.

But Salmon Woman is clever. She goes back to the village and
tells them her children will no longer live at the mouth of the river
but instead in the sea. They will go upriver once a year, and once
they are there they must not be fished. The salmon could only be
fished during the harvest moons, or everyone would suffer.

Bear and Salmon Woman had a tense relationship. In the original legend, Bear is the Salmon Woman's brother-in-law. In this
version Bear is her mother. Bear Mother thought she knew what
was best for everyone, especially Salmon Woman. She thinks she

knows what is best for her grandchildren, and it isn't being among the Salish. Bear Mother will always see them as traitors for what they did to her love and life. She will fix this.

Bear Mother goes to fish the waters upriver. Salmon Woman feels a tear at her heart. Another. Another. Another. She rushes upriver and sees her children floating by, lifeless. Sockeye. Pink. Chum. Chinook. Cutthroat. She reaches Bear Mother as she fishes Coho and sends his body down the river.

She begs Bear Mother to stop. She promises to leave the Salish people. She promises that her children will never know Salish culture. She promises to cut all connection with the people and stay out at sea herself.

Bear Mother is satisfied. She has successfully severed the toxic Salish ties. She has successfully protected her grandchildren and their future generations from the harm the Salish can bring. She leaves Steelhead in the waters. Scared and alone, Steelhead swims back to her mother.

Now, all of the Pacific salmon follow the ways of their ancestors. They spawn upriver and die each cycle. All except for Steelhead, who returns to the sea alone.

# ROOTS

I grew up in Carrollton, Georgia, right on the Alabama line. No other Native American kids that I knew of were in my school, and no one knew what to make of me. One girl told me once that I was mixed. She didn't ask; she declared. I tried to correct her, letting her know I was Native American. She told me that Indians didn't exist anymore.

⋙•

The house on South Valley Street in Port Angeles, Washington, was built around 1920. It was originally a single-story home with no indoor bathroom, built on nearly an acre of land. A creek ran down from the mountains and cut across the side of the property, watering the wild berry bushes that grew on its bank. My great-grandparents Lillian and Louis Kardonsky bought the home to house their family. Louis added on the upstairs so that they had a little more space. He also added an indoor bathroom, a new luxury for their family. He built a smokehouse that was constantly filled, preserving seafood to keep his family fed.

⋙

Lillian made most of the clothes that her family wore. She was a frequent customer of the JCPenney in downtown Port Angeles. They kept fabric stocked, and it was a location she could easily reach by foot. Once, when she entered the store, the woman behind the counter did not address her. Lillian gathered her intended purchases and waited for acknowledgment. It never came. The woman ignored her and helped everyone around her instead, never letting her eyes meet Lillian's. My great-grandmother did not relent, her famous temper being fueled to a brighter fire with each passing second. She had been called enough slurs that she could detect them, even if they went unsaid. When the burning temper became too much to contain, she acted. She did not leave or back away. Instead, she requested a manager from the woman. Lillian didn't move from the counter until one appeared. He recognized Lillian—she gave them plenty of business by clothing her family—and helped her check out himself. He didn't apologize for his employee's actions or punish her for her blatant racism. Port Angeles wasn't a big town; he likely knew Lillian had nowhere else to shop.

≫●

My family moved to Arizona the Saturday before my freshman year of high school started. I lived there for just under a decade. I moved from city to city after I turned eighteen, rarely staying in one place longer than a single lease term. Throughout my years in the desert, people confused me for other races, but at least they weren't surprised when I corrected them. Most White people saw me as Hispanic, and people of other races often thought I was the same as them. After a while I realized it was comforting for people to think they weren't alone in their cultural identity. I still couldn't keep myself from correcting them, even if it meant the distance between us grew a little.

I met other Native people in each place I lived. We crossed paths in student organizations, work environments, or hospitals. There still wasn't a connection. I had different experiences than them; I had grown up removed from my culture. I had never lived on a reservation or experienced life exactly as they had. It was enough that I was different, other. I didn't belong.

≫●

Leo, Lillian and Louis's son, sent his paychecks from the navy to them while he lived on base. He wanted to pay for the mortgage on the South Valley Street house, to make sure they never struggled to keep it. He ended up inheriting the home when they passed, both parents believing that he deserved it most having paid its mortgage all that time. He eventually left it to his own son, who moved in.

⇒•

My grandmother, Vivian, and her siblings were the first Native American children in the Port Angeles school system. It was not an easy integration. They were bullied and beaten daily by the other children, having stones and slurs hurled at them with no one stepping in. When Lillian went to the White principal about this, it was clear he didn't see it as severe. I wonder if he dared to utter the words "kids will be kids" in front of an angry Bear Mother trying to protect her cubs. When he finally agreed to act, his generous solution was to release the siblings ten minutes earlier than everyone else, to give them a head start on their run home.

It didn't always work.

⇒•

I graduated from Arizona State University, and my lease in Tempe was up the same day. My then husband and I stayed with a close friend that night before beginning our move to Washington the next day. We packed only what would fit in my small hatchback car. My books, which I couldn't bear to part with, were boxed up and shipped by a friend later. We drove for three days into the mountains in a car that struggled to go uphill. Still, we made it and I was finally back in my tribal homeland. In the beginning, it felt like coming home, even though I'd never lived there and rarely visited. My family members were welcoming, and the water and forest calmed the fluttering darkness deep within me.

However, I became disillusioned and was betrayed within a

year of arriving. My then husband cheated on me and lied to the other people in town. Not everyone believed him, but enough did. I wasn't skilled enough to help with tribal events, and I had been in cities so long that the limited entertainment of a small town got to me. The anxiety in me grew, as this place that had always felt like home in my mind began to shed the rose-colored visions I had coated it in. It wasn't quite right. I was welcomed by many, but I didn't belong. It wasn't quite home anymore.

⇒●

Something happened with Leo's son and the South Valley Street house. Some family members say he didn't pay the taxes on the home, others say he took a second mortgage out and couldn't make the payments. I was never close enough to that side of the family to ask without starting a fight. Regardless of the reason, the family home was lost. It sold at auction in 2017 for $71,000 to a couple from out of town.

⇒●

The Kardonsky-Cook siblings, as they grew older, continued to run into trouble centered on their race. Many places that were hiring weren't hiring Indians. Apartment landlords refused to house Natives as well. The White world around them still believed that Natives were dirty, lazy thieves. They had to lie about their race to find work, to find homes. Denying half of their heritage probably hurt and ached. It caused irreparable damage that could be seen long after these hard years had passed. Still, these were people raised by Lillian. They were taught, through words and example, to take care of their families first and foremost. Safety and security came before self-care, always.

⁂

I was accepted into the MFA program for creative writing at the University of New Orleans in April of 2018. I finalized my divorce from my cheating ex-husband that July and moved across the country in August to try and find a new home. This time, I took only what I could carry on a plane: two checked bags and two carry-ons. My aunt Gloria promised to ship my books to me when she could.

New Orleans was a great home between homes. It's a city of in-between and movement. People come and go. The city celebrates life, death, and weddings equally, and no one gets hurt feelings if you don't put down roots. I stayed until September 2020. The coronavirus pandemic struck me with not only sickness but clarity. The forced proximity it created between myself and the person I was living with made me realize I couldn't live there any longer. The city lost some of its luster when I couldn't go out to see the people in it.

I decided to move to Alabama to be with my parents. They drove to New Orleans to help with the move. We loaded our cars with only what would fit, with the front seat reserved for my two cats and the puppy I had adopted the month before.

⁂

The new owners of the South Valley Street house, who described themselves online as people who "love dancing, practicing self-realization, meditation, freedom, and investing," turned the Kardonsky-Cook home into an Airbnb. They named it "A Creek Runs Through It Olympic Mountain Retreat." It was one of the four properties they had purchased to rent around the Olympic Peninsula. The listing described the house as a "historic luxury two-story farmhouse" and charged guests $190 a night to sleep in the rooms where my family once lived.

A big selling point for their property was the creek that my grandmother and her siblings played in, that my mother explored before picking salmonberries from the bushes on its bank. They marketed the home as being close to the waterfront that my great-grandfather walked to every day for work. He was a long-shoreman and worked at the docks the entire time he lived there. His cat met him halfway home after every shift.

One review read, "It doesn't feel like someone fixed up a house and is renting it, it feels like someone's home."

—◈—

Vivian moved to California when her husband, Cooper, was assigned to a naval base in China Lake. It was a place where it wasn't bad or dangerous to be Native, and so she no longer hid her heritage. She told people that she was Native American. I imagine there was a spark of pride in being able to say it out loud after a lifetime of being ashamed or secretive about it.

But people didn't believe her. They told her that it was okay to be Mexican, and that she shouldn't be ashamed. These friends, most of them White, tried to be the best allies they could. They swore they wouldn't hate her for being Mexican, and every time she claimed her true identity they dismissed it. No matter how hard she fought, people refused to believe that she was Native.

꩜

I met my fiancé in Alabama. He's kind and funny. He is patient with me and treats me kinder than most other people have in my lifetime. A cliché I had never understood before was the saying, "Home is where the heart is." I understand now. I may never have full roots in a place, but I have them with him.

He has a network of friends who have grown up together and known each other for most of their lives. They are rooted, grounded in this place and one another. As we planned our wedding guest list, I realized that I didn't have many friends from the previous places I had lived. I rarely carried them with me as I moved; the baggage was always too much or too cumbersome.

One night, early on in the relationship, we were over at a friend's home when someone asked me about the places I have lived. I ran through the checklist, talking about how often I've moved. I made a joke about how often I left nearly everything behind, because as a joke it doesn't sound as lonely.

She told me, "You travel light; I like that," turning my lack of roots into a freedom.

꩜

The out-of-town couple eventually sold the South Valley Street house in 2022. No one I've spoken to knows who owns it now. Public records say that it sold for $439,000, which is likely more money than Lillian and Louis could have ever even dreamed of.

❧

My aunt Gloria was helping another tribal member distribute premade meals to the elders of the tribe. The elders came sporadically, which meant that there were long periods of downtime for the two of them.

The tribal member with her was from a different family within the tribe. He steered the conversation to tribal relations, and he said that plenty of people have a problem with the Kardonsky-Cook family. Aunt Gloria, a patient and gracious woman, asked him what he was talking about; our family members have almost always been involved in tribal politics, volunteered for cultural events, and attended tribal meetings. She asked him what in particular people had a problem with.

"Well," he said, "we all know that Kardonskys are only Indians when they have their hand out for something."

# SKINWALKER

It was 2013 and I was twenty years old. I walked on a broken foot for two days. I would shift my weight to the inside of my shoe and take shaky steps each time I walked. People told me I should seek medical help. I did anything I could think of to prove I was okay, that it wasn't actually broken. After all, I had only fallen out of an office chair. When I finally crumpled under the pain, I drove myself to the Phoenix Indian Medical Center in downtown Phoenix, Arizona. I had no insurance and it was the only place I could afford to go.

I limped across the waiting room. Dozens of Native faces watched me as I shuffled toward the intake window. I saw the weight of their long braids, black and silver and in between, and

I felt the fragile weightlessness of my close-cropped pixie cut. I tugged at the ends, willing my hair to grow out on the spot. When I got to the window, I was greeted by a woman my age. Her face was darker than mine. The way she paused when she looked at me suggested she was keeping track of that fact too.

She asked for my Tribal ID. She double-checked my registration. She asked why I was there. I felt the cutting double edge that question may have held, but I chose to only give her the medical reason.

"Something's wrong with my foot."

I was given a wristband. My vitals were taken. Every pair of Native eyes was on me, and it felt like they were waiting for something. Every pair of White eyes, largely belonging to the doctors and nurses, moved over me as if I was not there. I texted my Native mother and my White fiancé. I made a joke to make them feel better about letting me go there alone.

My mother was worried but ultimately counted on me being able to handle myself. My fiancé spammed my phone with message after message. He wasn't working that day, but instead was at home playing video games. He had pressed me to go to the hospital instead of classes and was thrilled when I said I would. He promised to have the apartment clean by the time I got home from the hospital. I would come back that day to an even dirtier apartment, with him high on the couch. It wasn't the first or last broken promise he made. A few years later we would be divorced, and I would be free of him. During this time, however, he was supposed to be one of the people I could depend on most.

In the hospital, I went to the emptiest corner of the packed waiting room and tried not to show my discomfort. I smiled, showing my teeth to those around me. They didn't smile back.

⁂

I was talking with my aunt Gloria on her porch in Sequim, Washington, one night in 2018. I don't remember what the bulk of the conversation was about, but I remember learning that other local tribes sometimes call our tribe "White Indians."

"White Indians? Why?" I felt the nervous smile creep onto my face. The kind of smile people get when a friend tells an offensive joke and they don't have the stomach to correct them.

"I'm not sure really," she said, long since dulled to the sting of the label. "We are pretty good with money, so that's probably part of it."

Silence overtook us for many drawn out moments. I thought about how little of my culture I grew up with. I thought about how I had to piecemeal our mythology together from scattered stories on the internet. And how I never learned the language. And how I barely knew any songs to welcome canoes home from a journey. I thought about how my idols growing up were not real Native women but instead cartoon caricatures that Disney made in the form of Tiger Lily and Pocahontas. I thought about how much other Natives disregarded me when they weren't from my tribe, as if I weren't Native at all.

"That's fucking stupid." I gave a hollow laugh as I said it.

⁂

The S'Klallam people were around long before European colonizers came to the coast. In our earliest told histories, we moved from village to village in our territory, keeping pace with the seasons. We hunted game and thrived from the fish and shellfish we harvested off of the coast. The crafters among us found strength in cedar. Strips of it were woven into baskets and hats, and the trees themselves were carved into canoes and masks. Cedar was chosen in part for its abundance but also for its connection with the spiritual world, and its longevity. The things made then were meant to stand the test of time.

≫•

There was no open chair in the waiting room for X-rays. Every seat was filled, so I moved to the opening that led to the hall. My sandal, which barely fit over my swollen foot that morning, was now too tight on my bloated skin. Every shift of weight sent pain rocketing up my nerves and I knew I had to sit. I pressed my back to the wall where I was and slid down, trying my best to keep my foot as comfortable as possible.

The other Natives continued to stare. Children who pointed in my direction and seemed to be asking about me were shushed by their elders. The mistrust made the air heavy. Despite my copper skin they still saw me as other, as outsider, as not like them.

The doctors, all White, glided past me in the hall. Not a glance was spared my direction. After an hour they called out number ten, and I glanced down at the plastic number I had been given: eighteen.

A passing nurse bumped my foot and I shuddered and gritted my teeth through a sharp inhale so I wouldn't scream. When the blinding pain subsided in what felt like minutes but was probably just a second, I focused on a man standing over me. The nurse who bumped my foot. He had an ice pack in his hand.

He said he was not supposed to give me anything since a doctor hadn't seen me, but he felt bad for taking my breath away. I took in his face. He was neither White nor Native, something outside the two major circles who moved in that space. He was the first person I was sure had seen me as just a person during that whole trip. I gratefully took the ice pack and tried to shrink further into myself.

⇒•

Eventually my aunt went to bed, and alone in her living room I was left wine drunk and stewing over "White Indian." *What the fuck does "White Indian" even mean? Who says that? Assholes.* I poured another glass of rosé and went back to the porch so that I could feel the cool air in my lungs.

The house was outside of any city, and the only light was from the stars and moon. A breeze caught the green scent of growing plants and pine trees and grass. I could feel the boil in my blood settle, leaving a thick, cooling rage. It was, at least, manageable.

"What do they know anyway?" I said to the sky. There was no answer except the doubtful echo in my mind. *What do they know? Do they know I was raised without drum circles? Do they know I have never pulled a canoe? Do they know that I don't like the traditional foods as much as I should?*

⇒•

The S'Klallam people first met European colonizers in the 1700s. But it was in the 1800s, after the establishment of Hudson's Bay Company trading posts, when the overtaking tendrils of White society increased dramatically. There was no treaty until 1855, when the Point No Point Treaty was drafted. It took many days, and the chiefs of the present tribes continuously voiced their concerns. Eventually they were worn down and the treaty was formed.

Later, the US government went against the treaty and tried to have our tribe sent to one of the reservations they had set up in Washington, including one that was along the Elwha River. The other was in what is now called Kitsap, farther south. They offered plots of land and $80 to anyone who would move to these locations. Members who moved to Kitsap became the Port Gamble S'Klallam Tribe, and those who moved to the Elwha River became the Lower Elwha Klallam Tribe. Some tribal members stayed, insisting that Jamestown Beach was where they belonged. They pooled together $500 worth of gold coin and purchased 210 acres along the water. There is where we staked our independence and became the Jamestown S'Klallam Tribe.

⇒•

After many hours a Native nurse led me back to the X-ray room. I hated the way she was talking to me. She switched between refusing to meet my gaze and appraising me, trying to judge the purity of my blood. I forgot the pain for a time and focused all of my attention on making her as uncomfortable as I was.

I pulled my phone out of my pocket as she set me up for the X-rays, and I began to take pictures. I smiled too wide and laughed and pretended the angle that she was making me position my foot didn't make me want to scream in agony. Through the vibrating pain I saw discomfort playing across her features and the whole show was worth it.

The news came that my foot was indeed broken, not sprained. I wasn't told this directly but instead found out as a soft Quick-Splint was put on my foot. The White doctor assured me that there was no way I could get my cast on that side of the hospital, and instead I had to use crutches to get myself to the other side. I had never used crutches before. The doctor laughed and told me that there was no better time to learn.

On the way to the room where I would get my cast, I had to pass through a large waiting room. It was packed full of Natives watching small, outdated TV screens. Every three or so steps I messed up and landed squarely on my splinted, broken foot. Before I was even halfway across the large open waiting area, I noticed a collective gasp each time that happened. I looked up to see a sea of eyes leveled on me. Most did not look away even as I matched their gaze.

I had become more interesting than whatever danced across those TV screens. I was the latest zoo exhibit, and I had to suffer this audience until I was through the hall. Part of me wanted to snarl or snap my jaws. I wanted to prove them right and turn into a beast before their eyes, one so feared and hated they wouldn't dare speak its name. I turned my eyes to the end of the hall and did not look away until I made it there.

꩜

I never escaped the pinpoint pain of the term "White Indian." I scoffed at it. I made fun of it and refuted it. I joked about it with friends and family to prove to myself how much I didn't care.

Ever since then, though, a stem of fear sprouts in me. When I hear someone move fluently through their own tribal tongue, I flinch at their authenticity. When I watch other Natives dance in elaborate ceremonial regalia, I swallow my awe so it can instead fester into shame.

This feeling of being fake doesn't influence reality. I am still dark enough to get stopped at airport security, followed around stores, stopped by police in border states, talked down to by people paler than me, and asked racist questions about where I'm from or what kind of magic powers I have. I still get treated like a liar or a relic when I tell someone I'm Native. I still feel a rooted, thrumming connection to the beach and the ground whenever I go home to Sequim, to where my tribe is. I still keep a mental record of all the stories I have learned, either from family or from historic documents. None of it validates me enough to remove the blight of impostor syndrome.

꩜

In 1953, the federal government decided that members of the Jamestown S'Klallam Tribe were not Natives anymore. This decision was an attempt to reduce the Native population through legalities. The rights granted to us were stripped again, and any hunting or fishing on the land granted to us by the treaty was now prohibited.

We did not take kindly to that.

All three bands of the S'Klallam Tribe—Jamestown, Port Gamble, and Lower Elwha—came together to fight for our given treaty rights and federal services in court. The case went through rounds and rounds of legal battles, continuously appealed to higher legal powers. Eventually, fishing rights were restored, but not federal recognition. It wasn't enough.

Other problems arose from the lack of federal recognition, which spurred the fight on. Healthcare and education access suffered without the previously given federal services. Moreover, tribal members wanted a more permanent guarantee of our fishing rights and land claims. In 1974, true, consistent effort went into establishing this recognition, although it wasn't fully achieved until February 10, 1981, when the case was resolved in the Supreme Court. The Jamestown S'Klallam Tribe became a fully recognized tribe and even registered a flag, being the smallest tribe to do so in the country. On it is our tribal emblem: the eagle—strength, power, and freedom—and the salmon—life, continuity, and adaptation—entwined in a circle.

⋙●

I finally arrived at what was apparently the only place in the hospital that could do a cast on my foot. The nurse was Native but welcoming; for the first time I felt something akin to comfort. She clicked her tongue at me when I stumbled and caught myself on my broken foot.

"That can't feel good," she said as she helped me to my seat.

"It doesn't, but I've gotten used to it over the past few days." I smiled at her.

She stopped moving. "You've been walking on a broken foot for days?"

"Yep."

"Wow," she moved again, prepping long strips of cloth in whatever material casts are made of. "You're pretty strong to do that."

I was more than a little caught off guard, but I simply thanked her. I took one picture as she was wrapping my foot and explaining what my healing process would be like. Later, when I showed my grandmother the picture, she paled and told me that the woman was the spitting image of my great-grandmother.

When my foot was thoroughly casted, I was wheeled back to my car. The kind nurse who looked like my ancestor asked me if I'd driven myself. I told her yes, and she looked worried but only told me to be careful.

I drove myself home.

⋙

Mentally, I've made a list of everyone who I think would possibly refer to me as a "White Indian." Some of them are specific names of the people I know do not like me or my tribe. Some of them are faceless groups, entire tribes on the Olympic Peninsula who notoriously do not get along with my tribe. I came up with a list of things I would say to them all, if I could.

Fuck you.

You don't have the right to define my identity.

I'm as valid as you are, asshole.

Do you know what "S'Klallam" translates to?

⇒•

Today, we have and operate eleven different enterprises, ranging from dental and medical centers to seafood distribution and business construction. Every building sports carvings that tell the stories of our people through fluid imagery. Between federal trust land and purchased land, we own 1,388 acres on the Olympic Peninsula and are by far the largest employer on that same land mass. We help tribal members get degrees and buy houses and enrich their lives and start businesses, all from funding generated by the tribal enterprises. It shouldn't come as a surprise. I don't speak the language, but even I have learned that the word *S'Klallam* comes from the Salish term *nuxsklai'yem*, which means the strong people.

# NATIVE ENOUGH

The first wave of guilt came with images of the protests against the Dakota Access Pipeline in 2016. The pipeline was constructed to transport crude oil through the Dakotas into Illinois. It was voted on and decided by White men and given permission not through voluntary easements, as was originally required, but instead through forced condemnations and evictions. The Standing Rock Sioux disagreed with the pipeline, as it was likely to destroy their ancestral burial grounds and taint their water supply with viscous, black poison. Their voices went unheard.

When the construction was announced to continue as planned, the tribe and their allies came together. People from across two hundred tribes and beyond to other communities came together to try and protect their water, their lives. They were met with forces from the National Guard and seventy-five other law enforcement agencies across the country. These forces used concussion grenades and automatic rifles against civilians. They spent hours shooting them with water cannons in subfreezing temperatures to try and make them give in.

I was working toward my bachelor's degree in creative writing at Arizona State University when videos, pictures, and stories from these protests started blooming across my Facebook feed. I saw Native people holding their ground and being ground down by the opposing police force. I saw them bitten by dogs and hosed down and maimed by rubber bullets hitting their faces and bodies, all while bright white words scrolled across the bottom of the video, explaining the situation and giving statistics.

I felt anger spill out of me. I hit the share button on nearly every post I came across. I spread awareness as best I could and checked in virtually to show my support for the protesters who were present. I wrote poems of rage and pain calling my people to action; they were published in the special edition of *RED INK Journal* that was dedicated to standing with Standing Rock. I saw my words stark against the white page:

*We are not what they paint us,*
*primitive, extinct.*
*We exist,*
*trapped beneath ivory*
*and barrier.*

I told myself that this was enough. I told myself that if I lived closer, I would have been there. I would have fought alongside the people who were being attacked by police dogs and maimed with rubber bullets. However, for me, getting there would mean buying a plane ticket and taking time off from school and work when I barely had the extra money for food. It meant the hardships of giving up paychecks and possibly even my job and my good academic standing. To get there was financially impossible, these poems and my online support had to be enough.

I was in an American Indian literature class in 2017, taught by a professor and full of students who could speak their Native tongues with ease. One of these students was a young woman, just a little older than me and in a graduate program. An entire class day was dedicated to a presentation she had to give.

She opened this presentation by introducing herself in her Native tongue. She then switched to English and began to educate the class on the unethical and possibly illegal Oak Flat copper mine that had been approved by the Arizona government, the Native land being written into the mine project at the very end and voted on too quickly. Natives and allies occupied Oak Flat, refusing to give way to the greedy destruction of even more sacred land. Video clips of hundreds of people dancing and singing played across the screen, cut with interviews by the protest organizers. They camped on the grounds and lived off the land, the way local tribes had done for lifetimes prior. Later that week, I received an invite over Facebook to claim a spot in that space and be part of history.

I never replied.

I could have taken a weekend off from work to take part; I

could have brought the ceremonial drum—hide pulled taut across the wooden rim and held in place by sinew twine laced across its back—that hung in my apartment gathering dust and put it to use. I didn't. I reasoned that I couldn't step away from my studies. I just knew that with all of those people at the event, they wouldn't miss me. I allowed myself to be told by my White then husband that whatever cause I wanted to support wasn't worth risking arrest or having a record as a disturber of peace.

"Especially not around here, with these cops." He ended his argument by brushing my arm and putting on a mask of concern.

"Yeah, you're right. Everything will be fine," I replied quietly. I had been terrified of Arizona cops since high school when more than one threatened to deport me during traffic stops. Being a US citizen didn't mean anything to them when my complexion wasn't light enough. I was always scared that they wouldn't bother with the paperwork and instead would take matters into their own hands to get rid of me.

"It's okay. They've got this. They don't need you there, Baby." He smiled. He then began to make plans for our weekend now that it was definitely protest-free.

I didn't listen while he mentioned the plans, and I swallowed the fear and relief that had melded into one lump of anxiety in my throat. I let others fight.

≳•

When I moved to Sequim, Washington, in 2017, I went with memories of totem poles and traditional carvings. As I drove past them, I felt everything inside of me align, if only for a moment.

I felt like I could be a part of the community here. I felt as if I could take part in tribal events and finally give my voice to my own people.

One of the first events I was able to participate in was welcoming the canoes home on Sequim Beach during the annual canoe journey. Nearly every year, many of the Pacific Northwest tribes come together to pull—the official term for rowing among the Native community—canoes from one tribal homeland to another. That year the hosts were the We Wai Kai and Wei Wai Kum nations, and the theme was Standing Together. Tribes from all along the Olympic Peninsula and British Columbia participated, with two different routes being taken along both coasts. The Olympic Peninsula tribes intending to make the full journey were to meet at Port Angeles and then pull across the water to Canada and continue their journey to the Campbell River. Each tribe is greeted at its neighbor's homeland with songs before they ask permission to come ashore. The Jamestown S'Klallam Tribe hosted a potlach dinner and ceremony for the canoes as they stopped along the way. It was the last tribal landing before the canoes reached Port Angeles and braved international waters. There were stories and songs and traditional meals.

I was entranced by the sight of the canoes coming in over the waves. I stood near the singers and reveled in the music and ceremony. I didn't know any of the words, but I was dying to sing along. I was determined in that moment to learn the songs so I could sing next time. The fact that my husband had refused to come melted from my mind when I was surrounded by the culture and life of my people. Later, Aunt Gloria would apologize for bringing me to one of the smallest ones she had ever been to.

I would repeatedly try to reassure her that it was beautiful, that I was proud to be there. I meant every word.

It was at this event that I got to meet various tribal members who held classes or led cultural gatherings. There were beading classes, training sessions to be part of the following year's canoe journey, drum circles, traditional food seminars. I asked everyone to keep in touch. I told them that all I wanted was to be involved.

The first requests I turned down because I wasn't really settled in yet. I just knew that they would have prevented me from doing my unpacking, which I was already procrastinating on, or from getting to spend time with my family, whom I already wasn't seeing. Then I got a job working as front-of-house staff in one of the restaurants in the casino, and my then husband worked in the same restaurant's kitchen. He didn't want me to go to events without him, and he didn't want to go out when we were off, so I stayed in. I turned down the first two drum-circle event invites on Facebook, which came from one of the cousins I was always trying to spend more time with.

I finally convinced him to go, telling him that it was important to me. The drum circle was a gathering where Natives from various tribes came together to sing traditional songs and play their handmade hide drums. It was a celebration of cultural pride. The one we went to was being held at the village of the neighboring tribe, the Lower Elwha Klallam Tribe. None of my family was able to attend, but I still felt an excited hum run through me as we walked into their recreation center. Groups of people were milling about, talking among themselves.

"I hate this," my husband muttered into my ear. His eyes darted from person to person, none of whom were looking at him.

"What?"

"We're clearly not wanted here," he said with a bitter voice.

Later in life I would file this under his narcissism. I would rec-
ognize the fact that this man-child couldn't stand being anything
less than the center of attention. At the time, his words struck
a well-worn chord of fear in me. What had just been groups
of friends became cliques, what had been curious gazes or an
indifferent lack of attention became glares and resentful silent
treatments.

We left before the music started. I clicked "Interested" on
every invite going forward, knowing I would never attend again. I
couldn't begin to escape the otherness he had cast me in, no matter how much I wanted to. He knew exactly which places to strike
to make me fold.

≫

After a few months I changed jobs and began working at the
Longhouse, the tribe-owned gas station. I worked from 5:30
p.m. until 2:00 a.m. Around the same time, S'Klallam language
classes were scheduled by tribal leaders. I got a Facebook invite
and accepted. I was excited to be a part of the resurgence of a language that was nearly dead.

The classes were every week, Wednesday, 5:00 p.m.

I could have gotten my schedule changed that day of the week
by my boss. I could have switched my days off so that Wednesday
was free entirely. I could have pulled the tribal citizen card to
make them work with me, especially for such a key part of tribal
culture.

I didn't. I apologized to the people running the class. I let it go. I never attended beading classes.

I never went to training to learn to pull the canoe.

I reasoned that I had never been able to grasp the language, or even have an idea of how it functioned, despite access to learning materials I'd gotten on my own. I explained to family that my hands shook too much to properly create works of beaded art. I apologized to the organizers of the canoe journey, explaining that I had never been physically capable and didn't want to slow anyone down.

Everything was an excuse. They felt so concrete, so real at the time. Now they are wispy, pathetic. I was terrified. If I participated in the world I moved closer to, then I would have to stomach the chance that I might fail at every task I tackled.

I didn't want to fail at being Native. Being Native to me then meant not only having the experience of all of these cultural things, but also being decent at them. I wanted to feel a peace in myself that cultural things brought me, but I had never felt so out of my depth. Failure felt imminent.

But I couldn't fail at something I never had the chance to try. So the excuses continued to pour from me, sweetly apologetic to hide the stench of the rotting fear that created them.

⸙

A few years went by. I got divorced and left my now ex-husband in the town where my tribe controlled most of the jobs; he could never tell me that I didn't belong again. I moved to New Orleans to obtain my MFA in creative writing. I had always been interested in writing and storytelling. It was one thing that came naturally to me, being able to bring together different points or craft words in a way that strikes the point exactly. It had always been an outlet for my emotions, though often hidden behind the veil of fiction or the indirectness of poetry.

New Orleans was far from the strong Native influences I had been surrounded by in Phoenix and Sequim. I was now in a city of transition, a permanently liminal space, a place where being a little outside of the normal cultures felt like the best possible option.

The first semester of this MFA program is also where my fear of failure was forcibly discarded. I had been late with assignments, forgetting things, or late to appointments with a workshop professor. She was not the type to let that slide. During my last meeting with her, when I stepped into her office fifteen minutes late, she told me we weren't going to talk about my story. We were going to talk about my self-destructive behavior instead.

"You wait until the last minute so that, when you turn in a half-done story or something that was clearly rushed, it's bad because you didn't give yourself enough time, not because of your writing skills."

I started to cry.

"You're afraid to give it your all and still not be good enough."

I continued to sob. Not because she was hurting my feelings, but because I had never had a piece of truth strike so deeply into the core of who I was.

"Stop crying, 'cause then I'll get started and we'll both be a mess."

I tried to laugh through the tears. I don't remember anything I said, but I'm sure most of it was incoherent. Later, I thanked her. If anyone asks, I credit her with my mental breakthrough that allowed me to write confidently from that point forward.

When I started writing about Native American issues in my first nonfiction workshop, people reacted. No one knew of all of the things that felt like common knowledge to me. I felt like I was a defining voice. It finally felt like enough.

Then I made the mistake of downloading TikTok, a social media app I'd made fun of long before I actually had it on my phone. Creators on the app make short videos of all sorts, and watching them was an easy way to pass the time when I was bored, especially while I quarantined during the coronavirus pandemic. I stumbled across #NativeTikTok and started watching the Native creators on the app. I was originally looking for jokes about White people, which I found.

I also found the videos of them showing off their traditional dances while outfitted in striking regalia. I heard their native languages flow from them like old, languid rivers. I saw the traditional food prep videos played over throat singing songs and stirring drumbeats. I saw them make jokes about life on reservations I had never experienced, and going to powwows I had rarely experienced—and even when I did, I'd felt more tourist than participant. Many jokes were about colonizers who claim to be Native because of some distant person in their family's history. The most common joke, and one I have told, is about someone being one-sixteenth Cherokee since their great-great-grandmother was a Cherokee princess.

I laugh at these jokes even as I worry that they would make that joke about me since I am one-eighth. I cackle and like the videos, and feel the flicker of pain in the back of my mind that screams that, if I ever had children, these videos would be about them.

And then I feel bad about calling myself Native in the first place. The pit remains in my stomach until hours after I have shut down the app and reminded myself of who I am and where I came from. I conjure up the carvings of my mental totem pole and try to slow my breathing until I can hear a solid, steady drumbeat in myself once again. On these nights I wonder if I will ever feel capable of beading or singing in Klallam. I wonder if I will ever feel Native enough.

# SALMON'S MEMORY

Salmon start to plan for their trip back to their spawning place when they are young. They form memories of how their home stream smells, so that when it is their time to journey to their death, they know the way. As long as the scent stays strong, they know that they are going the right direction; they battle the currents and risk death by many predators just to self-destruct in the manner they feel destined to.

❧

My grandmother Vivian Kardonsky Croft was Lillian Cook Kardonsky's fifth-born child. Vivian was raised to act White, as if her soul were made of porcelain. She attended the White church in Port Angeles with her family. Still, her skin was copper, and it did not go unnoticed.

Through the years she learned to reject the stories and the culture that ran in her blood. It fought, surfacing in every strand of her hair and darkening her skin each summer. Still, she tried to quell it; her mother's fear of them being punished by the world had morphed into a self-hatred that latched onto her bones.

Vivian grew into a beautiful woman. She was sixteen the first time she became a mother; the father lost to time. Later she would marry a man who hated Indians but could not resist her charm. He gave her another daughter when she was twenty, and then he left their lives forever. Through all of this Vivian held her head high.

⁂

Sometimes salmon lose their way in their trek upriver to their home spawning ground. Their memory isn't as crystalline as it has to be. Maybe their experiences at sea drowned out and stripped their minds of the smells of home. Maybe they never committed it to memory the way they were supposed to, and hoped it wouldn't matter.

When this happens, they backtrack. They reverse and search for a familiar scent, moving downriver until something feels solid enough to act on in that rushing current.

To support her family, Vivian started working as a waitress at a combination diner and dance hall in Seattle. One evening in February 1956, two young navy men strolled in. When Vivian spotted them, she poked her friend and pointed across the room at the more handsome of the two.

"I'm going to marry him," she whispered.

They laughed and Vivian went to greet the new guests. Six months later she was walking down the aisle toward that same handsome, smiling face. He was a Southern boy, and his name was Gary Cooper Croft. Strangely enough, the other waitress married the other navy man who had walked in that night. Vivian and Cooper's years of marriage were a whirlwind, with three children of their own to join the two daughters she already had. Cooper adopted and helped raise the two eldest daughters, even though they were not his by blood. They still call him Dad.

Cooper and Vivian were both stubborn and hotheaded and neck-deep in love for each other. A story that still gets passed around during the holidays is the time they fought over how dressing should be prepared for a turkey dinner. It ended when Vivian threw the turkey out the door. All of this happened between Cooper's deployments, when they lived in California on naval bases. Otherwise, she went home to be with her father and family in Washington. Eventually, once Cooper retired, they moved back to Cooper's home state of Georgia when their eldest—Vivian's third-born—was twelve years old.

Vivian continued to forge ahead, swimming upriver against society's current. She ran a home goods store in the small town of Bremen, selling decor of such a high quality that it never wore out. In the end, that was the reason the store went out of business. She beat breast cancer not once but twice, dealing with doubtful doctors each time. Even in her eighties, she scoured through scratch-and-dent stores and consignment shops looking for bargains. She kept an inventory in her garage and attic, and once a month pulled out her wares to have a yard sale, all to stay ahead of the rushing waters she still felt around her.

She overcame herself, too, and embraced her nature. Her eldest daughter stayed by the tribe and raised her children to take part in the culture and traditions. A drumbeat started back in Vivian's heart when her grandchildren began to learn the songs she never did. For the first time, with all of her children grown and developing families of their own, it struck her that she could not let her culture burn out. She began to collect pieces of the culture: a traditional "Indian yo-yo" made from seal fur and whale tooth, beaded medicine bags, a cedar hat woven by one of her nieces— items to try and make up the years and experiences she had let go. She was swimming upriver, going against the flow of time and purchasing back the years and self-love she had lost.

⇒•

Salmon is the only carving on my totem pole with predominantly red paint. Her original color was stripped, taken from her by her mother's fear. When it was redone, it was vibrant, but

angry. The black that outlines the other carvings shows steadfast-
ness, solidarity. Salmon is the only one who cannot accept what
she is. I wanted to tell her to stop swimming backward. I wanted
to guide her back to her home stream and remind her that her
past wasn't just anger, but I didn't want her to travel down that
path again either. Her home was filled with self-hatred and hard-
ship; Salmon is a symbol of sacrifice. She gave up herself and her
identity for security.

Sometimes, when salmon cannot find their original streams,
they will follow the school of salmon closest to them. They will
bed down and spawn in another river, and so they choose to let go
of their supposed destiny. They still die, but they allow themselves
to struggle a little less beforehand.

⇝●

My Salmon, Vivian, began to lose her memory in 2019. She
would forget conversations from one day—sometimes even one
moment—to the next. She had started a mental swim downriver, following its current, backtracking. In her old age she mel-
lowed some, the slice of her tongue dulled. In her backtracking
she found the familiar scent of anger. She latched on to it, and she
was intent in her mind that it was her way home. She mocked her
children and grandchildren; for a long time she belittled her husband who had a weakened mind from his own battles.

I wish I could have shown Vivian that she didn't have to find
that one river, that any path forward would have worked. Yet even
as I wished it, I knew it couldn't be true. She knew struggle and
anger and fighting against the world around her better than she

knew peace. Her swim ended in June of 2022. She went to what's next, and I hope that it is kind, and soft, and easy. Her color on my totem pole will always be a raging red from the time she spent in this life. Swimming upriver was always Salmon's destiny, and she embraced the challenge every step of the way.

# III

# Hummingbird

*The hummingbird represents beauty and joy. She is a creature of flight, bringing her closer to the cosmos with each wingbeat. She is constantly moving and is rarely seen at rest, preferring instead to perform her aerial acrobatics. Her heart is as fast as her wings and her colors are bright and shifting; they are colors that capture the sunlight in their iridescence. She brings love wherever she passes by.*

Hummingbird on my imagined totem pole is the most vivid in spring, with the smell of the surrounding new grass and the sun hitting her paint just right. Despite the storms she has endured, Hummingbird remains strong and vivid. Her wings are carved to show motion, a spirit captured mid-flight. Her stories are the ones that remind us how quickly things can pass by, and how fragile they can be if we do not fight to preserve them.

# A LEGEND OF HUMMINGBIRD

Every spring brings a special flower.

This flower is fragrant and gentle, its petals adorned with colors that shimmer in sunlight. She is the most beautiful flower that anyone has ever seen, though she doesn't think that highly of herself.

Everyone, people and animals, eagerly waited for this flower to bloom, Bear and Salmon included. They knew that, despite their differences, this flower meant that sunlight was about to stretch. This flower's presence meant that spring had arrived in all of its warmth and comfort. The flower brought joy because it was a messenger of sunshine and long days and new beginnings.

Raven sees this. Raven has taken many forms, and in this legend, she is a champion of the Salish people and the creatures that surround them. She observes the joy that this flower brings each time it blooms. The problem lies in the stationary nature of flowers. They are rooted, held in place by form. Raven knows that this flower could do more for the world if it were free to move across the land.

The next spring, Raven waits in the field for the flower to bloom. When the flower finally appears, she sits with her, and asks her questions.

*What do you value most?* Seeing others smile.

*What do you want?* To spread the joy of sunshine.

*Would you like to be free?*

There is no pressure to change, just an earnest desire to help her reach her fullest potential. Raven lets the flower make her own decisions, happy to accept whatever answer she gives. The flower, quiet and barely daring to hope, gives a gentle yes. Magic engulfs the gentle flower. The shimmering petals, delicate and fragile, are covered in a swirl and all the creatures that have gathered hold their breath, fearing that the flower is lost.

There is no flower when the dust settles.

In its place is the smallest bird in all of creation, no bigger than the palm of a man's hand. Her wings are the vibrant green of fresh spring grass. Her throat and belly are a deep red, the burning colors of the setting sun. Every feather shimmers in the sunlight, iridescent with the magic that made them. Her name is Hummingbird.

Hummingbird fluffs her feathers with pride but then shrinks again. She tells Raven she is unsure. She tells her that she has never been a bird and doesn't know what it is like to leave the ground. All she has ever known was being a flower. She is afraid.

Raven tells her that she was always meant to fly. She is meant to fly like sunlight flickering through the trees, to remind people of the swift magic in the air around them. Her heart was always Hummingbird, even though she had only ever known the form of a flower.

Hummingbird flies. She vibrates with joy. For the first time she can feel a drumbeat in her that had always tried to be heard, fast and excited and alive. Now she could beat along with her own wings.

Raven calls her over and gives her a task. She will be compelled to spend her life telling all the flowers how much joy they bring into the world and making each of them feel special and needed and important. She will have to dance in the sunlight to remind people of the joy that the light brings, and to make them pause to take in the beauty of the world, even when she will not be able to do so, because there will be little time for her to rest.

This was no challenge. Hummingbird would have done that all on her own now that she could fly.

# PORTRAIT OF A
# PERFECT NATIVE

I had the 1995 Disney movie *Pocahontas* memorized when I was young, to the point that even rewatching it as an adult I can almost recall it scene by scene. This is noteworthy because, until recently, I hadn't watched it in its entirety in many years—at least not sober.

I loved it as a child though. I loved watching the jewel-toned leaves swirl in the wind and the gentle magic that it suggested the Natives and the land had. I loved the music and the love story. I loved the way Pocahontas was fearless and strong and beautiful.

As a kid, I didn't know the historical events the film stole names from. I didn't know what whitewashing or stereotypes were. I never knew that Pocahontas was actually just a child, or that she was stolen from her family, forced to marry an adult White man. I never knew that she died because colonizers took her to England to display her like a circus act and she caught a disease she couldn't shake.

All I knew as a kid was that someone like me was on screen.

It was one of the only examples I had of what being Native meant in my small-town world on the Georgia–Alabama line. The music she sang to struck chords deep in me, rustling the feathers of the spirit I didn't yet know lurked there. These songs are what compelled me to revisit the movie when I got the streaming service Disney+ in 2019. I wanted to watch a beautiful, infuriating train wreck. I wanted to prove I had outgrown being hurt by a kids' movie.

So I started it. Within the first five minutes, there is the first use of the word *Indian* (*1:11*), the first use of the word *savage* (*4:29*), and the first mention of outright killing a Native person (*4:54*). None of these were the last instances.

I wished I had a drink.

＊

When I was around six years old, I dressed up as Pocahontas for Halloween. My grandmother on my dad's side, the White side, made me any costume that I wanted every year. That year I decided to mimic my own culture.

I had a headband with brightly colored beads sewn into it. My hair hung in two long braids down either side of my face. The material the costume was crafted from was meant to look like buckskin, with fringe on the sleeves and chest and hem. She even made me moccasins, with the same plastic beads that were on the headband. I remember feeling so proud of being dressed up as the perfect little Indian; it felt like I was finally doing something right.

꙳

Heroic John Smith sings about killing "Injuns" as he swiftly decapitates a mock-up Native made from a mop (5:07). This is a moment of the movie that has been etched into my brain since I first saw it as a child. I knew I was Native, and I was watching the valiant hero happily strike down something meant to represent my entire people. It must have affected me because I could always conjure this moment in my mind so clearly, even with years separating me from my last real viewing, but I don't remember ever reacting to it.

꙳

Whenever I ask my mom if I ever mentioned feeling uncomfortable as a child watching *Pocahontas*, her feathers ruffle in such a way that—if you did not know this Hummingbird—you would miss. It happens anytime I bring up the movie since I've become an adult. She always tells me that I loved the movie. She then always reminds me that she still loves the movie very much, despite all the controversy surrounding it.

I usually drop it at this point. Who am I to take away something that brings her joy, just because it doesn't do the same for me? Her response does quell any questions about why I was allowed to watch the movie in the first place: she's never seen anything wrong with it. I want there to be nothing wrong with it, but it's one point we will never agree on.

❧

The drumbeats that open "Steady as the Beating Drum (Main Title)" (5:37) are one of the parts of this movie that always makes me happy. The camera zooms over water and landscape that is colored in a magical pink and purple palette, giving the world an ethereal tone. Then there is a subtle wolf howl in the song just before the words begin and it drops us back into the painful Native American stereotypes this movie is constructed on. A man sprints by to blow his horn on a cliffside, and in doing so he gets within an arm's length of many deer. A classic Native American move.

The lyrics of this opening song are all about farming, fishing, and Mother Earth. There are also lyrics in Algonquian, which is the Native language spoken in the region where this movie is meant to take place. Unfortunately, none of the people involved in making this movie felt the need to keep track of what those lyrics translate to. The lyricist, Stephen Schwartz, assured viewers once in his online forum that they were heavily researched and definitely not made-up words, but he couldn't remember what they were exactly.

❧

When I was a kid, I was convinced that my hair was supposed to flow in the wind like Pocahontas's does in the movie while she is standing on the cliff when she first appears on screen. We were both Native, so it had to be true. She was the only Native woman I knew who had long hair like mine; both Mom and Granny keep theirs in pixie cuts and have done so all my life.

Even watching it as an adult, part of my mind still aches with hope that I will one day have hair that is well-behaved, even in a windstorm. The scene makes me give in to the urge to pull my hair into a messy bun. I need it out of the way so I can forget that I am not the perfect Native and watch Disney's version of this construct glide across the screen.

When Pocahontas begins to talk to her raccoon and hummingbird friend, I remember my tenacious attempts at talking to and befriending animals. Disney told me it was my blood-given right, and why would they ever lie?

⇀•

"Just Around the Riverbend" (12:45) is the least problematic song in the whole movie. Very few Native stereotypes here, it's just the adventure song of this Disney princess (because she is still a princess under the Disney marketing campaign, despite that being inaccurate in tribal leadership). Its fast pace and adventurous lyrics let the audience know that Pocahontas cannot be contained within the rules and boundaries of her home.

Like every Disney princess of that era, Pocahontas attracts various woodland creatures with her singing and magnetic personality. We see this first (13:40) as deer and birds and small woodland rodents gather along the shoreline to watch her race by in a canoe. It is unclear how much of this attraction is because she's Native and how much is because she's a Disney princess.

As she moves through the rapids, she sings about ignoring the sound of steady drums. Something clicks in a positive way that I did not expect: I, too, regularly choose to ignore stability in favor of the more fun and less guaranteed futures. For example, moving across the country multiple times without having jobs lined up, or getting not one but two degrees in creative writing instead of something practical, like architecture or marketing.

The melody slows and Pocahontas mournfully croons about whether she should get married or not. I have another revelation in my empty apartment: I think I have more in common with Pocahontas than I originally thought going into this viewing, including a poor outlook on marriage after my divorce only a year prior.

≫•

"Just around the Riverbend" regularly blares from my car's speakers. I may have avoided the movie, but some of the songs have found a permanent home in my music rotation. On any given day I can be found singing it as loud as I want, complete with big hand gestures that are probably not safe to make while driving. If someone happens to be in the car with me, I am much more subdued. I may even joke about the movie or liking the song because I am Native, because it's less awkward to make a joke than to explain that I'm just trying to preserve the one part of my favorite childhood movie that doesn't make me nauseous with anger.

≫•

Soon enough (*15:39*) Pocahontas introduces us to a new character: Grandmother Willow. She is a talking willow tree full of sage wisdom and spunk. As a child I thought being Native allowed me to talk to trees. I would press myself against them and try to hear a voice whispering from their branches or bark. Watching this scene as an adult, I realize that this belief of mine probably also stemmed entirely from this movie. At least it gave me a way into meditation, a way to calm my wild heart when nothing else would. Even now I can go outside and try to reach the roots of the plants around me with my soul. Something about that stretching invites calm.

⇛●

Once the White people are off their boat and rowing down along the shore (*20:00*), the natural world takes on more realistic colors and looks less magical. This has to be a deliberate choice by the animators to use only the magical palette where Natives are concerned, especially toward the beginning. White people are too practical and would never see pinks and purples where there would realistically be more toned-down greens and blues, obviously.

This change in art style is followed by a prolonged example of Native fire magic (*23:09*) when the village elder / medicine man tosses some herbs onto the fire and the smoke takes on the shape of soldiers who turn to wolves. No wonder when I was little everyone my age thought I was some sort of mystic being, including myself. Disney told us so.

I didn't know how to be Native, but I knew I needed to prove my heritage to people. In middle school I would clip and braid feathers and leather strips into my hair. I didn't know how to handle my desire for isolation that I now know is just part of being an anxiety-ridden introvert, so I made people want to stay away from me on their own. I would tell them that I could speak with my ancestors, and that I would curse them and their whole family if they didn't leave me alone. Most of them believed me, and those who didn't had no desire to be associated with me anyway.

Now I wonder if my ancestors looked at those moments and sighed in disappointed ghost tones about the strange little mixbreed their line was ending in. I wonder if they are prouder now of the person I've become. I wonder if they watched as I tortured myself with a Disney movie just to prove a point to no one.

"These White men are dangerous" (*35:50*). This is the truest statement in the whole movie.

"Colors of the Wind" (*39:20*) is a whole song just telling John Smith how incredibly wrong his mentality is. The music is so good I can't help but love it. However, the lyrics are so full of stereotypes that I think I'm a bad Native if I don't tell every rock hello and ask for its name.

The magical colors also return in this song (*40:14*), because now the White man is seeing the world through Native eyes, I guess.

I stopped my first rewatch of the movie just before the song "Savages (Part I)" (*1:03:49*). I didn't have the heart to face it alone that day. And I didn't have anyone else around to watch it with me. Everything else, every other gross inaccuracy or stereotype can be turned into a joke or made funny, but this song can never be funny. It hurts. It makes me angry, stirring that pitch that rolls underneath my consciousness and bringing it to a boil. It always has. It is the most dramatic, striking part of the movie and I can't bear to watch it.

The lyrics make my stomach turn. The White chorus calls the Natives evil, red-skinned vermin. They claim their enemies are barely human, more akin to devils. Savages. They call for their death again and again and again.

When I did finally watch it, I didn't allow the tears to roll down my face. I held them, making my vision watery. I tried not to listen and instead focused on the animation.

The colors used in the animation during this entire song are darker, more contrasted. The purple and red palette is still there, but it has a sharper edge to it now. Instead of mystic colors they become colors of bruises and blood, colors of war.

I remember as a child watching that scene and feeling that everything about the song was off. I didn't like what the White men were saying about my people, but I didn't know how to express that emotion, that doubt.

Watching it as an adult, I found new reasons to be angry. Whoever wrote the lyrics tried to make both sides seem in the wrong, but that's hard to do when the Natives have cause. Their land is being destroyed; their people are being attacked and killed. Even when trying to make them balanced, the writers couldn't bring up the vitriol on the Native side that comes in buckets from the colonizers.

When I finally went back to the Disney+ app to finish the movie, I updated my profile first. Part of that was adding a profile picture, for which I had the choice of a plethora of Disney characters. I sought out the copper skin tone of Pocahontas and selected it. I don't know if I'll ever escape that association; the only difference is now, whenever people ask or point it out, I make it a joke instead of taking it seriously. I make the choice knowing that part of me hates myself for it.

⇒•

"Savages (Part II)" (*1:06:36*) is the big finale song. Musically, this is one of the most beautiful songs on this entire soundtrack, but I can't bring myself to ever own it or put it on a playlist. The lyrics make my stomach drop and bile rise into the back of my throat.

The red sky that opens this song is such a strong symbol of war and death. Having the villain Ratcliffe be the first character we see against it is fitting; it adds to his evil demeanor.

Pocahontas, even when distressed, commands the presence of Magic Wind and all the wildlife, as seen in her race toward the battle during this song. Deer and birds move alongside her, granting her nature's swiftness or something like that, I'm sure.

Ratcliffe and chorus scream about my race being demons and their desire to kill us all. His eyes have literally gone red to match the sky at this point. I have to remind myself again that this is a children's movie.

A line about destroying the race completely plays, and I pause. I don't remember that line. I wondered if I just didn't hear it when I was younger because of the swelling music, or if I blocked it out so that I could still enjoy one of the few movies that had people like me on screen. Also, good on Disney for acknowledging the genocide that the American government still won't.

Pocahontas puts her head over John Smith's to keep him from being killed (*1:07:37*). I don't want to get into the gross number of historical inaccuracies this movie possesses, but this is one I still have to point out because it is extremely false and dumb. It's based off a story the real John Smith told that no tribal member agreed with. What is worse is that it fits this narrative so perfectly. That act of bravery, the Brave Warrior Indian Princess protecting the Righteous White Hero, brings the swelling song to a halt, leading to complete musical silence. This makes the moment even more captivating. It creates a natural place to hold your breath as an audience member. The tension is addicting and makes this scene enthralling to me even though I hate everything about it.

The rest of the movie doesn't matter. It's about John Smith and his struggles, and that was never the part I cared about. I finished watching but nothing could shake me out of my burned-out feelings.

⇒•

As the credits played, I felt so sad for young Leah. She, I, watched this over and over and over until every line and motion was memorized, until every stroke of color was emblazoned into her, my, mind. The word *savage* is used forty-six times, and other derogatory or demeaning words toward Natives ("dirty shrieking devils," for example) are used twenty-four times. As a child I took every one of those gut punches just to enjoy the only slice of representation I connected with, in life or on screen. And I did so while singing along.

# A WRITER WHO CAN'T READ

ʔaʔcłtiŋ'íxʷəŋ'—to be speaking in a Native American language, talking Indian. {*ʔaʔcłtiŋ'íxʷəŋ' či! // Speak your native language!*}

Hazel Sampson was the last native speaker of the Klallam language. Her mouth learned to form its shapes and syllables before she was introduced to English, long before my own mouth existed at all. Her eyes could graze the written word and she could understand it without pause. She died on February 4, 2014, at the age of 103.

Hazel was from a time when the S'Klallam Tribe was whole,

before they were split into three. Later in her life she was rela-
beled as a member of the Lower Elwha Klallam Tribe. According
to those who knew her well, none of that mattered to her. She was
S'Klallam; the colonizer splitting of her tribe didn't change her
identity.

I sometimes wonder if she would be ashamed of me if we
had met.

> ʔaʔkʷinit—to protect, take care of, nurse, adopt
> someone or something. {ʔaʔkʷinit cn. // I take care
> of it.}

A Klallam dictionary was published November 14, 2012. It was
created by Timothy Montler, an emeritus professor at the University of North Texas, far from the coastal home of the language
he worked to preserve. It is a heavy book, filled with notations on
who worked on which part. Montler worked closely with some of
the last living native speakers of Klallam, including Hazel, though
she declined to be part of it in an official capacity. The entries
span over a thousand pages, all carefully curated to protect a legacy that didn't belong to the man who was the driving force to
create it. I admire his drive and his passion for preservation, even
though it is another spike of guilt that sometimes makes me feel
like I am not doing enough.

Technically, now, Klallam is a dead language. A dead language
is one that has no community, even though some may be taught
to speak it. People can form the words and reanimate what once
was, but Klallam has long since breathed its last natural breath.

Still, Montler's efforts and nursing of this cause kept it from going extinct and becoming nothing more than a crumbling memory, the way so many languages have.

ʔáʔi—to imitate, to mock. {ʔáʔi cn. // *I'm mocking.*}

A writer who can't read is a sorry sight. When I don't understand a language, I want to skim over it. I want to let my eyes gloss over its twists and bends so that I do not have to feel lesser for not understanding. I have never been able to accomplish this. No matter the language, I fixate. I try to determine what each word means and how those curves and edges are meant to be pronounced. This is especially true for Klallam.

I have never been able to grasp the way the words of the Klallam language function. It is a garland on street signs and walls around Sequim. It is a marker on every newsletter and update sent out from my tribe. Whenever I see it, I try to will it into something understandable. I stare and hope for the words to shift around and suddenly make sense, as if my blood is enough to grant me literacy.

Still, when it is spoken to me, the speaker may as well be silent. When I see it written, it looks more like art than script. The curls of the letters and quick dashes of accents create something beautiful and striking. It stirs me in the same way the stars do. I am smitten and I want so desperately to understand more, to navigate the patterns and relive the stories they tell.

All of that adoration brings me no closer to understanding.

I cannot pronounce a single word of the S'Klallam language, not even those that appear on these pages. I have crafted them through copy, through a careful study of the dictionary entries so that each letter is correct. Some small part of me hopes that this will better my comprehension, but it feels like an imitation, a mockery.

>    **ʔaʔkʷúsc**—teach me, teach you. {*ʔaʔkʷúsc u cxʷ? //*
>    *Will you show me how?*}

The introductory pages of the Klallam dictionary include guides on both the common and unusual characters and how to pronounce them. The character I have come across the most, *ʔ*, is described as "being produced deep in the throat, right at the vocal cords." It is called the glottal stop. It is the noise you make when you voice catches in your throat, or you interrupt yourself. The dictionary describes it as being the sound between the syllables of "uh-oh."

If I try to say the word for "teach me": *[Catch], ah, [catch]* . . .

The character *kʷ* is pronounced like the beginning of "quick," with rounded lips and the tongue rolling from the back of the mouth.

*[Catch], ah, [catch], kweh, ooo, ess* . . .

The letter *c* is a trick in the Klallam alphabet. It is not the kicking sound at the start of "catch" or "county," or even the hiss at the end of "truce" or "ace." It is pronounced as *tiss*, with the tongue behind the teeth as if you have just finished saying *rats*.

*[Catch], ah, [catch], kweh, ooo, ess, tiss.*

Even when I have been shown how to say each part I am still lost in the pronunciation. I cannot even ask to be taught.

ʔáwənə—to not exist, be none, nothing, nobody, no
one. {ʔáwənəʔ sx̌číts kʷsə ŋəˀnaʔ či sƛ̓aX̌ʼəmʼúcəns. //
*My daughter doesn't know the Klallam language.*}

Four generations ago, my family only spoke Klallam. My great-
great-grandmother, Nora Cook, lived with my great-grandmother
and her family. She watched as Lillian refused to teach her children anything but English, and still she refused to allow English
to pass her own lips.

Lillian's choice was one made out of fear. She wanted her children to be safe, and being safe to her meant being White. She
couldn't change their features, but she could control their culture with a heavy hand. The language was one of many things
they did not inherit, and it was left to decay alongside traditional
songs and rituals. Because of her decision, my grandmother Vivian never learned the language. My mother never thought about
it. Now I am left to put the pieces together, with a fear of failing
that makes my hands tremble as I do so.

caʔčáct—to continue on, move ahead, move on.
{*caʔčáct cn. // I moved ahead.*}

Today there are a number of high schools and middle schools
on the Olympic Peninsula that are teaching Klallam as a second
language. I am mostly happy about this fact. The thought of young
minds absorbing this part of the culture so that it doesn't vanish
or become a relic of lost times brings me a level of peace. Many
may not be fluent or may forget large chunks of the language in
a few years, but for now they know it. For now, these classes, and

classes taught by the tribes to whom the language belongs, serve as respirator, giving the chest of Klallam a synthetic rise and fall.

I wish I could be fully happy. I want so badly to let go of this guilt; this greed that makes me want to say that I should know it before they do. I am the one who has neglected to learn so far; I'm the one still standing in my own way. Klallam has already become relic, and I am scared that my attempts will morph it into an accessory rather than a respected cultural aspect.

I often think about how Hazel might have felt when she saw the dictionary completed. On the one hand, she contributed to its pages, even if it was indirect. She was part of how Klallam was crystallized and preserved. I imagine her worn hands running over the pages and looking for the entries she helped create. I picture her with a smile on her face.

Then I think about how it must have felt when the novelty wore off. How did it feel to be the last authentic inhale of a language? I wonder if the weight of being the end of an era stooped her shoulders or tugged her brow downward. I wish I could ask her why she didn't teach her children or grandchildren the language she helped preserve later in life. I fear that I know the answer already, that it would be the same as Lillian's: *safety*. There's a safety in vanishing what defines you as different from your oppressor.

ʔəw'k'ʷ—to give out, be all gone, be depleted, be done, no more, finished.

# HUMMINGBIRD'S MOVEMENT

Hummingbirds know where they've been. These tiny, prismatic birds keep a record of what flowers in their territory feed them best, and the quickest routes to get there. The strongest of mind have consistent mating songs, never warbling or missing their notes. Their minds are mostly hippocampus, the part of the brain dedicated to learning and spatial memory.

⁂

My mother, Kristy Croft Myers, is Vivian and Cooper's eldest. Whereas Vivian was raised purposefully against her Native American heritage, Kristy was simply raised without it. Her family never took part in the cultural activities as she grew up. But her heritage still shows in her features: thick black hair, tan skin, high cheekbones. For Kristy, her heritage was never something to fight against or embrace. It simply was. Even when her mother, Vivian, began to embrace the culture more it did not affect Kristy. She was an adult by that time, looking toward her own future and not anyone's past.

Hummingbirds learn quickly. They not only know where they've been, they commit it to memory within an hour. They have to. Their lives and bodies move at such a fast pace that they need high-energy food sources, and to accidentally go to an already depleted flower could be fatal. The hummingbird feels as though its life depends on getting things right the first time, and that the weight of their survival depends on them being the fastest and the smartest, and from learning from their past mistakes.

Kristy married young a man who gave her two children before they were divorced. After that, she met Randy Myers, a Georgia-born man with two kids of his own from a previous marriage. They knew each other for two weeks before they started dating and dated for two weeks more before they were married. Eventually they had one daughter of their own: me.

The righteous temper of the women who came before her missed Kristy. Instead, she is kind, and passionate in that kindness. When her children were growing, she taught them to care for all living things, showing them life through the lens of her spirituality. She cared for and helped raise Randy's two children from a previous marriage, just as he did hers, attending games and recitals, resolving sibling wars. Their house became the center of nearly every family gathering, hosting over forty people each Easter and Fourth of July. The seating spilled from the tiny kitchen and dining room into the living room and out the back door onto the deck. There were children darting between people and dogs begging and many conversations overlapping, trying subtly to be the most prevalent. She hosted them all with a laugh on her lips, one that could be heard from any point of the house.

Hummingbirds cannot walk. Their feet are tiny and not meant for anything but perching and small movements to the side. This is the tradeoff they made for their sky-dancer mobility. Feet that permitted normal movement on the ground would take away from their acrobatics. Now they must move at their flight speed or not at all. There is no in between, only flitting from place to place, using their speeds to survive and provide for the families they create.

While she is not as hotheaded as her mother and grandmother, Kristy is just as hardworking. When her youngest child was only five, Kristy worked three jobs, two of which had her waiting tables in a small Georgia town where tipping was not always the most generous. She, like the women before her, wanted her children to have a life better than her own. Hummingbirds are constantly in motion, rarely seen at rest even during their nesting season. My Hummingbird, my mother, is no exception.

Now she works at a Baptist church in Alabama and feels at home. She runs a program through that church that teaches English as a second language to those who want it, free of charge. It started as her simply assisting the teachers, but eventually she took on the role of teacher herself, practicing with Zoom lessons with me and my dad. Alongside the English classes, she assists in organizing mission trips all over the globe for preachers in her department, helping reach out in her way so that the world can have more light.

⇒•

It is hard to get a hummingbird to slow down. Their wings are what give them their name, flapping so quickly that the beats run together into a hum. Their hearts move at an even faster trill, with some beating as fast as 1,260 beats per minute. It is all in the name of visiting as many flowers as possible, and of coming home to roost sooner than later.

⇒•

When asked about her heritage, Kristy is proud to be a Native American woman, though not everyone can see it. Once, when she had stopped at a red light in Georgia in the late 1970s, a man shoved a flyer for the Ku Klux Klan in her face, pitching the benefits of membership for her family. She crumpled it up and threw it back at him, letting him know just how wrong he had been to assume she was White. Yet he did. Many have over the years. It is not that her features are subtle, but when so far removed and the bloodline is thinned, people don't see it as clearly. The totem poles don't support her spine the way they do for others. Kristy is proud to be Native, but when asked if she cares deeply about it, she can only joke and dismiss the question. She may not hear the drumbeat in her heart, but it is there. I hear it for her. It beats as clear as the hum from a hummingbird's wings.

# IV

# Raven

*The raven is the trickster of the Coast Salish tribes, often known for her creativity and humor. She is intelligent and easily bored, which often leads to mischief. She brings necessary changes to the community while holding tight to its symbolism and tradition. She ensures that her voice is heard and reminds all that the world is full of surprises.*

Raven sits at the top of my totem pole. I picture her wings and feel a click in my soul, a sense of rightness. I have known since I was young that this would be my symbol. When I close my eyes and slow my breathing, I can picture each curved line of her carvings, from eyes to beak to wings. The top of the totem pole is the newest and clearest, but also the part that leaves no room for the future. She represents the end of an era: the last, defiant wingbeat of a culture.

## A LEGEND OF RAVEN
## STEALING THE SUNLIGHT

Raven has many legends among the Salish people. This is the beginning. In the original legend, Raven is a man. In my version, Raven is a woman.

In the beginning, there is darkness. The trees are there. The water is there. The light is not. Raven, like the other creatures of the world, pays this no mind until she sees light for the first time. It is a glimmer from inside a Salish man's cabin. The only light the world has ever seen.

Raven flies closer and perches on the windowsill to watch. Inside there is an old Salish man, with a frown etched into his face. In the original legend, he has a daughter, but in this story he is alone. The house is filled with boxes and baskets, but Raven is fixated on one particular box, the one in the man's hand. A powerful glow radiates from this box, giving light and warmth to the home. But as soon as Raven observed it, it was gone. The man had shut the box's lid and tucked away the light.

Raven forms a plan to get that box.

Raven is not an altruistic soul. She does not want to bring light to the world, or to brighten the lives of others. Raven will become a collector of shiny things, of trinkets that sparkle and glow. This light will be the first in her collection, the shining star that starts it all.

In this version, Raven shifts into a lost child. She exudes innocence and trust through her form and relies on the loneliness of the man and the human desire to care for another. She approaches his door and cries.

The man is overjoyed. He dotes on her and gives her the best life he can in this world of darkness. She is allowed to play with most items in the home, but the box with the light is strictly forbidden. She cries and wails and squawks with the stubborn desire of a toddler. The man does as many fathers and grandfathers have always done; he caves.

Raven marvels at the brightness of the light from the moment the box opens. Carefully, the man places the light in her lap to allow her to play. Raven grins up at him and for a moment the home is at peace. Then Raven begins to transform. Feathers sprout from her skin and her grin morphs into a beak. Before the old, lonely man can react, Raven grabs the light in her beak and flies up through the smoke hole of the home. She does not look back at the man whose secrets she has taken.

The world instantly changes. Reflections begin to dance off of the rivers. Trees and mountains throw their shadows as Earth inhales its first taste of sunlight. The world wakes, and Eagle is awakened with it.

Eagle is larger than Raven. He is more vicious and combative. Eagle's goal is to prove his power through force, and Raven undermines him in every place she can. He is constantly searching the darkness for her form and failing to catch her. Now his target is illuminated and clear.

In her joy at success, Raven does not hear the beating of massive wings right away. For a moment, she does not feel the air grow dense with the fear and awe that Eagle invokes in the creatures of the world. It isn't until he gives an early, triumphant call that she swoops just out of his reach. In her sudden movement, the ball of light slips. When she grasps it, it splits in two. Half of the light falls to the ground and shatters.

Half of what hits the ground bounces up and hangs in the sky, pockmarked and rough. The other half shatters into millions of tiny slivers that float up like dust and settle in the darkness. These become the moon and stars.

Eagle continues to chase Raven. He is relentless in his desire to suppress her. They have flown for hours, and Raven begins to tire. She knows that as long as she carries this light she will be a target. As long as she shines and he stares she will not be free of him. She curves toward the sky and flies as high as she can, with Eagle trailing behind. Raven gently releases the light, letting it hang high in the vast silk of sky, toward the east. She flies down with the light behind her. Eagle is blinded and loses her in the chase. Raven lands on the trees below, breathing easy now that she is away from Eagle for one more day. She watches the first rays of sunlight break through the branches. It wasn't what she intended, but the light is still, in a way, hers.

The forgotten Salish man is angry. He cries at the loss and betrayal. He covers his eyes and curses his weakness for sharing what was meant to be his alone. When his breath is finally even again, he moves his hand. Sunlight streams through the windows and the smoke hole of the home. The world outside is vivid and bright and welcoming. He knows in that moment that this was always meant to be, and his light will live on longer than ever.

# UNREPORTED VIOLENCE

When I was sixteen there was a White boy, Jonathan. His face was all angles, with dark eyes that had an edge to them, even when he smiled, as if waiting to pounce. He was tall and broad, a natural build as he would rather spend his time playing the piano or violin than working out or playing sports. I was so in love with him it hurt. At first the pain was all my own creation, my heart striking against my sternum when he was near, or my lungs shriveling because he took my breath away.

I'm not sure when he first started hurting me.

⌇

Native women are in danger simply by existing.

At the time of writing this, Native people made up 3.6 percent of the missing persons cases in the United States according to the National Missing and Unidentified Persons System (NamUs), while making up only a total of 2.9 percent of the population. Even this disproportionate amount of missing people is most likely on the low end of the real numbers, since many cases go unreported. Even the ones that are reported do not always make it to federal databases because of the tenuous relationship Native reservations have with their local governments, and the blur of responsibilities and jurisdictions that tension creates. We go missing more than we exist, and elected officials make our bodies political.

⁂

As Jonathan and I grew closer, somewhere between friends and more, he began to touch me more, wrapping an arm around my waist or grabbing me to pull me closer to him. Without my notice these connections evolved into something rougher. At one point my right bicep, my left forearm, my right thigh, and both of my sides just under my ribcage all sported bruises at various levels of healing. They all were the shapes of handprints and fingers. A friend taught me how to cover up the bruises with makeup, but I never told her who had made them. The one on my bicep is partially visible in the only photo I have of my Junior Prom night, a shadow I forgot to hide. I blamed a different friend to protect Jonathan from my parents.

When I finally confessed my feelings for him, it was in Spanish over a text. *A veces te odio pero a veces te amo.* Sometimes I hate you but sometimes I love you. My brain shut off then; the only words I could think were *fuck* and *why* and *please* on repeat. I knew he didn't speak Spanish, but I also knew he would look it up. Still, saying it in English would have been too much somehow. He came back with a text asking if I really felt that way. When I said yes, he told me I would make a great back up, someone to give him affection and attention in between girlfriends, and that he was glad I was so easy for him to have. I convinced myself that these were good things; that somehow this made me one step closer to whatever it was that I wanted.

➳

Some people are actively fighting to keep Native women alive. Most of these efforts to bring this issue to light are spearheaded by other Native women, trying to protect one another. One such woman is Annita Lucchesi, a cartographer and descendant of the Cheyenne. She is working on a database dedicated to cataloging missing and murdered Native women across the United States and Canada. She has a total of over 2,700 names so far. Native rights activists have created #NotInvisible to spread awareness of the atrocities Native women face, to bring to light the violence that continues to be neglected by authorities on all sides. In the 2021 report, there were 5,203 reports of missing American Indian and Alaska Native women and girls logged by the National Crime Information Center. The US Department of Justice's federal missing persons database, NamUs, logged only 246 cases. We just want to survive and thrive without having to look over our shoulders, but no federal justice department seems to want to help. One of the symbols for the #NotInvisible movement is a red handprint painted over the mouth, to demonstrate the violent silence inflicted on our women.

≫

The last bruises Jonathan ever left on me happened the day he tried to kill me. We were swimming together in a pool of a vacant house in my neighborhood. Everything was fun; we were making jokes and laughing in the relentless Arizona sunshine. He moved close to me, and I felt a trill in my chest. I held my breath as he reached toward me. I thought he was going to kiss me. Instead, he put his hands around my throat and forced me under the water.

It wasn't like the moments of betrayal that happen in the movies. There were no scenes of my life flashing before my eyes, or memories of him and I up to this point playing over sad violin music. At first there was just denial. *This is a joke. We were just laughing. He'll quit soon.* Then his hands tightened, and my lungs began to sting. The laughing was gone. I didn't know what went wrong. It had to have been something I did. I somehow managed to spoil the fun and ruin the joke.

≫

Statistics are stacked against women in general, especially when it comes to strangulation.

One of four women experience domestic violence in their lifetime.

Sixty-eight percent of those experience near-fatal strangulation, 97 percent of them by the very hands of someone they love.

Thirty-eight percent of those strangled reported losing consciousness.

Seventy percent of them believed they would die.

The ones who manage to walk away are marked with red eyes, swollen lips, scratches, bruises. They often have difficulty speaking, swallowing, and breathing.

⇒•

Jonathan had locked his arms and wasn't showing any signs of moving, and my lungs were starting to complain. I couldn't see his face, just his silhouette against the unforgiving sun. He didn't react when I tapped his arms to signal that I needed air. I tried to move to the surface, and he pushed me farther beneath the water, refusing to let me have the satisfaction of breathing. The sting in my chest grew into a constant burn as my lungs began to demand air.

My primal instincts finally kicked in: *survive.*

My hands had been loose on his, not really trying to do anything in the naïve faith that he would stop of his own accord. That hope vanished. I dug my nails into the backs of his hands and pulled hard. I thrashed and fought again toward the surface of the water, toward the rippling sun and the too-dry air I craved. His grip tightened further and began to crush my throat instead of just holding me in place. His body was locked in place. I could feel the tensed muscles as I scratched and pulled and hit. For someone who hated the gym, he was incredibly strong. The long fingers that danced across piano keys felt like marble, unmoving as they locked around me.

My brain shut off; all I could think was *Fuck* and *Get Away* and *Live* on repeat. The water filled with bubbles from my frantic motions and the sun disappeared in the commotion. I lost track of which way was up. The worry about upsetting him evaporated. The notions of love and friendship and winning him over were gone. In that moment all of that mattered as little to me as I ever did to him.

꙳

In 2021, the date May 5 became federally recognized as Missing and Murdered Indigenous Persons Awareness Day. This recognition was part of a grassroots movement trying to raise awareness of the crisis that Native people, especially Native women, face by just existing each day. The day was chosen because Hanna Harris's birthday was May 5. Harris was a twenty-one-year-old woman who went missing in July 2013; her family reported it but felt only indifference from the police. The family gathered volunteers and formed a search party of their own. It was this group that found her body after three days. She had been murdered.

Native women are murdered at a rate more than ten times the national average in some areas. Across the country, we experience an overwhelming amount of sexual violence, with more than 80 percent reporting assaults. Again, the statistic is likely low, since not everyone reports the violence taken against them. Some may keep quiet out of shame or fear or a nauseous mix of both.

꩜

In that pool, my vision tunneled down. The chaos of bubbles I had created with my motions was blotted out by darkness creeping in like the tide around my eyes. A dangerous calm overcame me as I relocated the sun above me, distorted by the ripples in the water. My throat felt as if it was collapsing and my insides felt like they had been set on fire, but I could think in full sentences again.

*If I don't get him off of me, I am going to die.*

It was the clearest thought I had ever had around him. It repeated in my head, looping over and over for what felt like minutes but must have been less than a second. It was the only thing I knew to be true in that moment.

I regained control of my legs and brought them up, putting them between myself and Jonathan, planting my feet on his chest. My body was curled tight, and his grip did not relent. *If I don't get him off of me, I am going to die.* I built up what strength I had left and kicked as hard as I could, pushing his chest with both of my feet. His nails scratched my neck as he was forced to let go.

I broke the surface and drank in air, heaving as my entire body shook. I pushed my hands against my chest to try and calm my heart, which was still frantic with fear. My muscles tensed as I remembered that danger was present. I spun around, looking for Jonathan. I wanted to place him. My primal, fear-scattered brain wanted the predator in sight. My hormone-drunk brain still just wanted to see him, to see his face. I wanted to know if there was anger there, or confusion, or something stranger I couldn't guess at.

He was out of the water putting on his shoes. His face was blank. It was as if a computer model hadn't been given an emotion to process yet. His dark brown hair fell in a perfect line across his forehead. Not a single aspect of his appearance was out of place. He looked at me and those cutting dark eyes threatened to take away what breath I had gotten back. For a moment my pain subsided. Then a coughing fit hit me as I tried to breathe and the pounding pain of my throat reminded me of the fear I should be feeling.

"I need to go home," he said. He watched me for a moment before walking around the side yard and through the gate to the front.

I climbed out of the water and lay on the warm flagstone that surrounded the pool. My body was still shaking. I felt cold despite the sun beating down at over one hundred degrees. Now that I was safe it was as if my brain went into autopilot. *Relax. Gather your senses. Move along.* I stood, finally stable enough to do so, and pulled on my shorts and T-shirt over my bathing suit. I grabbed my phone and sent my mom a text.

ME: Taking Jonathan home. Should still get home before
    you do.
MOM: Okay sunshine!! Drive safe! I love you!!
ME: Love you too

I gathered my things, keys, wallet, phone. The sun shining did not shake my chill, despite the sensation of water droplets evaporating from my skin. I went around to the side gate and slowly pulled its latch high, out of the gravel at my feet. Normally the sound irritated me, but I heard nothing. I shuffled to my car, which was beaten and abused. He was waiting, leaning against the passenger door. I unlocked it, and he got in without a word or pause. When I would tell my story years later, even now, people asked why I took him home, or why he assumed I would after what happened. I don't have any answers besides a shrug and being young and dumb. This should have been the interaction that would teach me that I don't owe anything to the people who have hurt me. It wasn't. However, it would be the moment I look back on as the very start of a turning point, because turning points often start at rock bottom. In that moment it was rock-bottom weakness and the fear of losing what I thought was something good in my life that made me avoid confronting him. It had yet to sink in that I would have been dead if it were up to him.

So I drove to his home, in silence except for the alt-rock radio. He got out of the car, winked at me, and told me we would do it again soon. I still don't know if he meant swimming or attempted murder. I watched him walk to his house, a grand building isolated on more land than his family needed or used, no neighbors in sight. My hands shook on the steering wheel as I left his driveway and headed home. My throat hurt too much to sing to the radio like I usually would.

≫•

A report from the Urban Indian Health Institute gathered information on cases of missing and murdered Native women across seventy-one different cities. Most of the cases occurred after 2000. These are the statistics from the cities they covered that I've lived in or near.

New Orleans, LA: Missing: 1.

Seattle, WA: Missing: 7. Murdered: 38. Total: 45.

Tacoma, WA: Missing: 13. Murdered: 10. Unknown: 2.
Total: 25.

Tempe, AZ: Murdered: 2. Unknown: 1. Total: 3.

Tucson, AZ: Missing: 1. Murdered: 30. Total: 31.

Phoenix, AZ: Missing: 8. Murdered: 6. Total: 14.

—

I never reported my attempted murder to the police out of shame. Shame that it happened in the first place. Shame that I was too dumb to stop hanging around him after the first bruise appeared. Shame that I took him home afterward. Shame at the fact that I used makeup to cover up the handprint-bruise necklace from that assault for weeks, never showing anyone.

The few friends who I eventually told didn't believe me. They never thought he was capable of such a thing. They thought we were so close. They thought I was exaggerating or maybe I dreamt it. Only one, the friend I was closest to, didn't outright deny it, but he asked me if I had done something to make Jonathan angry.

Sometimes I look up my would-be murderer online to make sure we are far apart from each other. His friends and family all gush on his social media about what a good man and husband he is. His White wife never has bruises in their pictures.

After learning the statistics stacked against Native women and seeing how he moves in a whitewashed world, I wonder if he would have attacked me if I were White.

# SCALPING KNIFE
# TURNED SCALPEL

Genocide is defined as the deliberate and systematic destruction of a racial, political, or cultural group. In many cases, this means murder by an oppressive force, such as the United States government using treaty meetings to pass out blankets they knew would inflict disease and kill Native populations. This happened in the early days of manifest destiny, which was the belief that American settlers moving to the West was justified, inevitable, and sanctioned by God.

In recent times, the destruction is more subtle. The scalping knife that was a tool of genocide has become a scalpel, carving apart families and the women who could create them. Unlike the scalping knife, which left ragged edges, the scalpel cuts in precise lines. The blade still leaves scars.

≫∘

It started with the stealing of children by the United States government, which began officially in February 1959, under the name The Indian Adoption Project. Its official purpose was to lift the obstacles that prevented Native children from eligible adoption during a time when "race matching"—placing children with families that most closely matched their own race or skin tone for visual cohesion—was a priority. The goal, on paper, was to give these children a better life, a chance at a White family life.

It looked like charity work if no one paid close attention. Reservations and other Native communities had almost universally poor living conditions and high unemployment rates. These same communities had some of the lowest literacy levels alongside some of the highest rates of sickness and poverty. It was easy for government officials to address the "Indian Problem" by stating that Native parents were incapable of taking care of their children. Seemingly no one questioned why the communities were in such terrible states to begin with, which was largely due to lack of government support and isolation, which hindered their access to resources that were readily available to other communities.

Then the media took hold of the idea. Articles with titles such as "My Forty-Five Indian Godchildren," "God Forgotten Children," "Indian Children Find Homes," and "Interracial Adoption" encouraged White couples to adopt and—in their minds—save

Native children. Hundreds of White families favorably responded to this wave of media.

The Child Welfare League of America, the oldest child welfare organization in the United States, actively worked to reduce the Native community through adoption as well. Native children were only considered adoptable if they had one-quarter or more Native blood, the ones who could continue carrying the race forward. Anyone below that line was unacceptable. This was another form of assimilation. Move tribal citizens away from their homeland when they are children. They would never know their culture and therefore wouldn't pass it down to future generations. A slow, suffocating death for the race.

In the late 1960s, Bertram Hirsch, an employee of the Association of American Indian Affairs—a nonprofit dedicated to preserving culture and protecting sovereignty of the Native nations—conducted research around the subject of Native children in foster care. He found that between 25 and 35 percent of all Native children at the time had been removed from their families and placed in adoptive homes, foster homes, or institutions. Approximately 90 percent of those children were being raised by non-Natives.

Even today, many Native children are taken from their homes on baseless claims, such as uninvestigated accusations against the parents' sobriety or care level. Other people on the reservation or in their community commit to being foster parents, but the children are still sent off to live with White families, far from their culture and home.

⇒●

I tried to sell my eggs, my potential children, once.

The fertility companies who buy them have to use the term "donate" instead of "sell" because it is illegal to sell body parts. It is the same way that a person "donates" plasma for money or gift cards at sketchy centers once or twice a week. I am familiar with both because during my first marriage to a White man, we never had enough money for rent and selling my body in these forms became a regular conversation. One month we were desperate enough for me to try.

The process for donating eggs is fairly straightforward. First is a fertility screening, where a doctor examines your ovaries and other reproductive parts. Second is a medical screening, searching for infectious diseases, drug use, and other general health issues. These are followed by genetic and psychological screenings, where it is determined if either your family genetics or your mind and motivation are too twisted to produce a child. If, after all of that, you are found an acceptable breed, the actual donation process begins.

This process is a series of birth control pills, hormone self-injections, more tests, and finally a light sedation and egg retrieval, which is done in thirty minutes or less.

I didn't make it past the genetic screening.

Being a minority was a plus. Being Native American specifically was a huge plus. Plenty of people want Native children, but there aren't that many mothers willing or able to part with them.

Coming from a family with diabetes was a negative. More problems that fell into the not-suitable genetics category were a history of addiction in my family, multiple cancers, and my own mental disorders of anxiety and depression. A large number of these strikes against me are associated with Native populations and Native genes. The same genes that made Native kids so popular for adoption or as egg implants were the reason they were ruled out.

I left the experience somewhat relieved. I would have to find money elsewhere to pay my rent, but at least I didn't have to be poked and prodded for months until they took what they wanted from my body.

⇒●

Stealing children became harder in the 1970s and 1980s because they weren't being born as frequently. The average number of children per Native woman dropped from 3.29 during the 1970 census to 1.30 at the time of the 1980 census. This was in large part due to the forced sterilization of Native women during that time.

The Indian Health Service (IHS), the national program that to this day provides medical care for Native people, sterilized one in four women between the ages of fifteen and forty-four they treated in the 1970s. Twenty-five percent of Native women were denied their choice to create life, and often illegally.

There were meant to be regulations in place, set times between when a consent form was signed and when the procedure actually happened, to ensure that the patient was aware of exactly what was being performed and what it meant. A report released by the Government Accountability Office on November 6, 1976, confirmed that IHS didn't follow these regulations. The forms were not up to standard; patients didn't fully understand all of their options. In some cases, a full hysterectomy—the removal of the uterus—was conducted without the patient's knowledge.

Doctors who performed these procedures often cited the lack of care they believed Native mothers capable of. They were backed by the approval of the United States government. The Family Planning Services and Population Research Act of 1970 subsidized sterilizations for patients who received health care through IHS. These medical professionals were being paid to eradicate a race one womb at a time.

⇒·

I have never wanted children. When I picture my future it almost never contains raising little humans into functioning adults. I have self-diagnosed tokophobia: the inexplicable, irrational fear of pregnancy and childbirth. On severe days, the thought of something moving inside of me, forming into life, makes me want to vomit.

While I was in Washington and had access to tribal health care, I decided to obtain a long-term birth control solution. With this solution, I wouldn't have to add another reason to worry to my always-growing list of worries, especially as I started a new chapter of my life: moving across the country to attend graduate school.

I did my research and decided on a copper IUD. It lasts ten years, isn't hormonal, and doesn't need any maintenance. It was perfect.

My normal doctor wasn't available for my visit, and instead

I got an older doctor. She was White, like my normal doctor, but had a grimace where my doctor had a gentle smile. Still, I explained my plans and my concerns. She nodded along. I told her that I was moving in five weeks, flying across the country, and I needed to have it done before I went. She continued to nod.

"Well, do you ever want kids?" she asked with an impatient tone in her voice.

"Um, no, probably not. I'm not sure, but I really don't think so." I laughed, nerves bundling in my stomach, reacting to an unseen fear.

"Well, I'm asking because we can always sterilize you."

I stammered, confusion slowing my tongue.

Sterilize. Like an animal. Like a sick or diseased thing.

She pulled out a pamphlet and showed me how easy it would be to guarantee I never had the chance to have children. Just a cut of the tubing that connected my ovaries to the rest of me. Two snips to end any chance of life.

I felt sick. It was a swirling mix of the usual nausea at the thought of going through pregnancy and childbirth, and a new, sad bitterness at the words being said to me. I'd read so many articles and stories of women fighting for their right to their bodies. Many women, White women, had to claw and beg and fight to convince a doctor to "tie their tubes." They had to prove that they truly didn't want children, and that their husbands don't want children. Even then, the doctors would sometimes refuse them the option, even if they were steadfast against creating life, in case they changed their mind in the future.

I expressed a reservation, a dose of indecision, and this woman tried to press me into it anyway.

I let her finish her presentation, which she delivered with the most excitement she had shown so far, as my twisted gut turned from confusion to indignant anger.

"And it would all be at no cost to you," she finished.

"I appreciate that, but I want to stick with my plan of the copper IUD." I could feel that my voice had gone cold. The smile I had before still sat on my face but was devoid of any emotion.

"Oh. Well, we can do that if it is what you really want." She opened up a calendar on her computer and scrolled to the end of the month. "We can do it in four weeks."

"Why such a long wait?" I was getting on a plane in five weeks. I was not planning on coming back anytime soon. If there were any complications, I would be stranded without insurance.

"That's just when it will be best to do the procedure, with your cycle."

I brought up my concerns again. She wouldn't budge. She said that was the only time she felt comfortable moving forward with my choice of birth control. Numb and worried but out of options, I agreed, and the date was set.

The following week I saw my normal doctor for an unrelated checkup. Once the core of my visit was out of the way, I mentioned my IUD insertion procedure and how far off it was.

"Do you know why she set it for so far out?" my doctor asked, confusion spreading across her face.

I relayed the conversation I had with the other doctor and was met with an exasperated sigh.

"If you want to reschedule it with me, we can get it done two days from now. There's no reason to make you wait."

I agreed, and as promised, two days later I was walking out of the clinic with the birth control I had chosen. No complications, no excess pain. Now, I think of all of the Native women who never got the chance to have children, either from their own forced sterilizations or from being kidnapped or murdered. I think of all the children with Native blood who were in danger or stolen from their homes. I can't help but clutch my abdomen, even though I wish for it to remain empty. I can't bear the thought of giving up what was forced from others like me, no matter how little I may want it.

# A LETTER TO MY SEVENTH-
# GENERATION DESCENDANT

Dear Great-Great-Great-Great-Great-Granddaughter,

You probably don't exist. I have never wanted to be a mother, and that will probably never change. Still, every time my tribe reaches out to those of us pursuing higher education, we are asked what we are doing to plan for the future seven genera-tions; at least once a year my thoughts are brought back to you. In my mind each year when I conjure you, you look like what I imagine my daughter would look like. You have a healthy col-lection of freckles dusted across your high cheekbones, black hair that hangs in curls, bright blue eyes, and skin just a shade lighter than my own. You are beautiful. Then I have to remem-ber that you would not be my daughter but someone much more removed. A generation is measured as an average of 25 years, so seven generations create a gap of 175 years. At that thought my image of you pales; your face loses the angles I know come from my Native blood, and your hair fades into a golden brown. You are still so beautiful, but you look nothing like me.

Many Native American tribes practice this seven-generation philosophy, starting with the Haudenosaunee alliance of tribes that inhabited northern New York. For as long as Native history has been told, we have planned to better the world decades down the line. In the past, this has dictated fishing and hunting regulations, relations with neighboring tribes, and keeping the fire of culture alive. Now the question is asked of those of us pursuing higher education. It is geared toward facilities and infrastructures, toward progress in every field. It is still a matter of sustainability. Instead of leaving enough fish, we need to maintain access to other resources for tribal members—medical, welfare, and otherwise. Instead of keeping peace with neighboring tribes, we need to throw our voices into larger politics, aiming for a global scale. My role in this is that of record keeper and storyteller. I am here to keep the fire of culture from burning out. It is an overwhelming task when I realize you might know nothing of it.

In seven generations from the year I was born, the year will be 2168. Writing that out it doesn't feel that far away, but I know it is. The world has changed so much in my lifetime, and that's just under thirty years so far. I have no idea what the world you would be living in looks like, let alone how you would choose to make your place in it. My tribe has taught me to plan so far in advance, but all I can think about is dilution. By the time you are

born, the Jamestown S'Klallam Tribe could be as much a myth
as the sea-wolf or the thunderbird is to us now. I like to imagine
you are one of the flames dancing to keep us relevant. Even then,
when I imagine you making a drum or learning a song to welcome canoes home, it feels like a lie.

My cultural world is governed by percentages and numbers
and blood, and I realize now that you may not understand.
There are blood quantum laws in place; an archaic, controver-
sial system that tells us whether or not we are Native American. These laws were originally designed and enforced by the
federal government as a way of choking out tribal citizenship. It
may be difficult for you to believe, but they are now upheld by
tribes themselves because some tribal members fear that without them, the culture will die. With these laws the race will die,
but that is the unspoken truth of many Native communities. We
have been told for so long that we are history, some of us have
decided we would rather become it than let our culture thin out.
Both argue for survival, simply in different ways.

I am one-eighth Jamestown S'Klallam, 12.5 percent. According to these blood quantum laws, this means that I will be the
last member of my tribe in my line unless I choose to have children with another tribal member. However, there are only a
handful of families within the tribe, one being my own. So, if
I ever did have a child, the chance that she would have enough
Native blood is narrow. This means that, if you exist, you will
likely have less than 0.1 percent S'Klallam blood in your veins.

When I think of my imaginary daughter, only one generation over this invisible line, I hate the idea of blood quantum. I
could teach her every aspect of my Native American heritage,

bring her to every event, teach her every story. She would still be legally White. It may give her and her family, and eventually you, more privilege, but it creates a break. The stories that mean so much to me might just be stories to future generations, hers or yours. The drumbeat in my chest could easily soften into a normal heartbeat in those who would come after me.

And so, though I hate to admit it, when I think of you, I understand the laws. I do not know how anyone with so little connection to my culture could claim to be a part of it. I know this comes from being a tribal citizen with no cultural upbringing. I cannot imagine you would be raised in our culture—even if I know my own children would be—because I only have the framework for how I was raised. I disgust myself by drawing my own line and putting you on the other side of it, but it is my truth. Numbers do not really matter to heritage, but I have been told for so long that they do; it's hard for me to see things any other way. Every day I carry my tribal member card with me. At times it felt like my only connection to something I felt so deeply about, since I grew up with an emptiness where our songs and stories should have been. My ID is a federally recognized little rectangle of plastic, a badge of being an Indian, for better or for worse. While that piece of plastic may not determine the contents of the soul, it has shaped the lens through which I see mine.

Seven generations before I was born, the year was 1818. There were some interactions between S'Klallam people and settlers, but no major trading posts had been built on the Olympic Peninsula yet. The treaty that would eventually be signed had not even been drafted. There is a good chance my ancestor seven generations ago never interacted with a White person in her lifetime, and yet in eight short generations a White person is what her descendant will legally be. I do not know anything about my ancestor, but I know she must have been taught to plan for me the way I am taught to plan for you. I often wonder if she ever considered that her tribal lineage would end in seven generations, but I know she probably could not bring herself to that conclusion. When she thought of me, she likely thought of someone as dark as her. She probably pictured a family teaching the traditional ways to fish, or a young woman learning bead-work and lore. I wish I knew her name. I hope that, if you are there, you will know mine.

That is my plan for the future seven generations. I will write our stories and records. Despite the daily pressures I face as a woman to create a family, it is not a role I feel am meant for. I may not be willing to give my body to the future in the form of offspring, but I can give my mind and my research. My paginated creations are likely the closest I will get to children, to legacy. Yet every time I write about my life, my tribe, or the history of Native Americans in general, I think about you.

I like to imagine you as the family record keeper, like me. I picture you viewing Facebook photos of my life the same way I organize printed photos of the lives of those who came before me. I picture you with a network of family, asking older relatives who each person is in a photo or video, and keeping all the notes collected somewhere safe, maybe alongside the things I will write. I wonder if you see yourself in me as you rifle through the thousands of photos on the cloud, or if I am just another face in a collection to mention in passing. I hope that you are still taught to plan for the future seven generations, and that you try to keep the stories of our people from burning out, even if you do not hold the flame yourself. If you ever do exist, I wonder if you will read this and know I did my best to plan for you.

Some nights I think I want to take a step toward creating a future that has room for you. I talk to myself in excited tones about what my children would possibly be like and how I would raise them. When I have a partner, we sometimes talk about the perfect combination of our two selves and construct pretty scenarios around these little dreams. Our children would be smart and beautiful, and we would raise them to be kind and happy. However, the conversation, whether alone or with another, always ends up at the same place. I reiterate how I will probably never have children; we talk about how much time and energy and patience that requires. I love the thought of you and all of my theoretical descendants, but I don't know if I am the person who can give so much of themselves to another. I want to travel, to be free to move and work as I please. I want to be able to devote myself to my art or to a cause without the worry that I am neglecting the person I am pressured by the world to love the most. Some call these selfish excuses to opt out of motherhood, but I do not need to explain myself to them. I just wanted you to know that I do think of you even knowing that, because of my decisions, you are probably not there.

With Love,
Your Ancestor

# THE SOUND OF THE END

Deep sounds often unnerve us. Human hearing has a low-end limit of around 20 hertz (Hz); infrasound exists below that frequency. It is a range of sound that we feel instead of hear, a pressure in your mind. Infrasound is the force that urges you to act even when you're unsure why. It is an indication of disaster and danger. These low rumbles are present in many things that frighten us down to our most beastly, primal minds, the place we go when survival is all we can think of. Infrasound is a mark of the things that make us feel mortal and powerless. Tigers, tornadoes, large ocean waves, earthquakes.

The Cascadia Subduction Zone is a fault line that runs seven hundred miles from Canada to California. On its back are mountains and coastline, cities and towns and campgrounds buzzing with people and creatures who call those places home. Beneath it shift two major tectonic plates, one that moves the Pacific Ocean and one that moves the land itself. These plates are pressing into one another, grinding in imperceptible tones. It is a game of chicken that neither plate wants to lose, and so they continue to push when pressed together, shoving the people on the coast closer and closer to the ocean. We are overdue for something to give, as it has done before.

The last time this fault line shuddered was January 26, 1700, more than 300 years ago in an estimated 243-year cycle. The Earth shook and an entire forest of red cedar, a wood famous for standing strong against the elements, was just one of many places ruined within minutes. This ghost forest, still filled with gray, weak corpses of these trees, is only eighty-three miles from the tribal center for the Jamestown S'Klallam Tribe, my tribe.

≫•

For ten thousand years people with blood like mine built a thriving community on the Olympic Peninsula. Even when colonizers came, tribal members gathered gold coins from their own pockets and bought their land outright so that they could persist. The tribe has since built building after building, health-care clinics, housing, and cultural galleries. We are the largest employer on the entire peninsula. Our songs and stories echo off the mountains that surround our home. Tribal designs and carvings can be seen down the coastline and throughout the towns of Blyn, Sequim, and Port Angeles. We have roots as deep as the mountains that grow with every push of the tectonic plates that are at war. We are entrenched.

But there are only 542 of us left, and dwindling.

≫∘

Infrasound is most commonly associated with a feeling of dread.

An experiment was conducted at a concert with 750 attendees. Infrasonic notes were woven into parts of the music alongside the classic melodies of Debussy and Philip Glass. The change was subtle and secret. The crowd was unaware of their lab rat status, and many reported strange feelings during the notes they could not hear: shivering, a gut feeling of something being wrong, and a sense of having lost something or someone that you cannot replace. They claimed that an extreme anxiety overtook them, as though they had perceived a danger for which they had no name. For some it may have felt like the end was a looming, invisible wave waiting to crash onto them.

The fear that infrasound creates does not always have to stem from this existential danger alone. Many people argue that because of the way infrasound resonates with the human body it can have adverse effects. Vladimir Gavreau, a scholar of sound in the 1960s, became obsessed with this unheard range only when he and his team felt nausea as the infrasonic waves passed through their bodies. There were reports of motion sickness, as if the ground itself rolled beneath their feet.

≫o

When the ground shakes beneath the Olympic Peninsula, the area will be devastated. Very few people have prepared for this, since an earthquake has not happened in hundreds of years; they have become lax and unwary. Homes that are not ready will tremble into pieces. Family pictures will crash to the floor of my aunt's apartment and hand-picked vegetables will roll off the counters of my cousin's kitchen. This will not be the worst of it.

Following the initial earthquake, solid ground will act is if it is water. This is a phenomenon called liquefaction. This pretender tide will bubble and roll and disregard the decades of progress built on its back. Experts have mapped out where the high danger zones are, the ones most likely to lose form and liquefy. The tribal center, the casino, the health clinic, the Longhouse, the beach where canoe landings are celebrated, the housing for tribal members, all of it rests on high-risk land. Land that is likely to rush out to sea. The water that comes to take its place will most likely destroy whatever else is left. I wonder if a single totem pole, carved from red cedar chosen to stand the test of time, will remain standing once the earth and sea settle.

≫o

Of the 542 tribal members left, 297 are one-eighth S'Klallam. Because our blood-quantum laws mark the cutoff for being a tribal member at one-eighth, these are the last in line. I am one of these 297. Unless our future children are the product of two members, the child's blood will be considered White despite its redness.

There are talks of plans for the Tribal Council to change this again, to bend the rules so that color can be seen in those who come next, like they did in 1994. However, if the laws ever do extend to include those who are one-sixteenth S'Klallam, it will likely be in twenty or thirty years, when the numbers have dwindled further.

My nephew is one-sixteenth S'Klallam and only seven years younger than me. He dropped out of high school and fell in with a bad crowd, but he has grown now into someone who aims to be better. The life he has led has never been easy, but financial troubles made it harder than it had to be.

In twenty or thirty years he may receive the benefits that his mother does; that I do. He may finally have the ability to get semi-consistent medical care, or the funds to buy Christmas gifts for his siblings or to put gas in his car. He may be able to rely on a network that has built-in care for tribal members to help him pay housing fees or deposits. He may finally be able to afford to go to college.

But he won't get the incentives and rewards for grades in high school. He can't go back and undo the decisions he's made because he knew his family could never afford to send him anywhere. He cannot go back and learn to be Native, to live for the honor of those who came before him. By the time they may change these laws, my nephew will be forty or fifty years old and he will have settled into the until-then-fact that he is White. What good will being S'Klallam do him then, if his own children face the same circumstances he did? Why haunt him with ancestors he never knew to care for?

Ghosts are sometimes made of infrasound. The watchful eyes of those who came before us are sometimes just the thrum of our environment. The way these low frequencies roll through human bodies do more than give us shivers and chills and dread. At around 18 Hz these waves match the resonant frequency of the human eye. The resonant frequency of an object is its own natural vibration, the speed at which it exists in the world. When this frequency is matched it knocks the object off balance. When the human eye is met with vibrations around 18 Hz, the vision begins to blur.

Vic Tandy was a researcher in an engineering lab. He would experience moments of depression, of chills and dread. Once at his desk he saw a dark figure lounging out of the corner of his eye, some entity waiting for him to notice. He would turn and the ghost would be gone. Others reported the same; the building grew into its haunted reputation.

Eventually Tandy found the ghost generator, a "noiseless" fan that created infrasound between 18–19 Hz. The frequency was low enough to be a standing wave; instead of creating a moment of fear, the wave stayed and continued to pass through the researchers. Dozens of pseudo ghosts were created every day by vibrations of the eyes. I wonder if any were haunted by images of their ancestors, if a researcher's brain morphed those vibrations into an ancient face that wore a mask of cold disappointment. I wonder if they were just on edge or if they feared for their lives.

⇛•

The earthquake and tidal wave that will most likely destroy my tribal home will take an estimated thirteen thousand lives and injure many more. It will down power lines and wipe out lineages. It will leave the people without basic electricity, water, and sewage services for at least a month, likely longer. It will be over a year before the hospitals function again.

There is no timeline on when the canoe journeys will start again. There are no numbers for when the next drum circle will be held or how many will participate. There is no guarantee that the Makah, a neighboring tribe at Neah Bay and the most vulnerable group to all of this, will even be around to attend.

The Makah tribe's reservation engulfs the very tip of the Olympic Peninsula, seventy-five miles from the nearest full-service medical facility. They are a whaling tribe that has fought valiantly and sacrificed much to retain their culture. When the 1855 treaty with European colonizers was drafted, their cultural rights were held hostage. To retain whaling rights they had always accessed, they had to cede the title to three hundred thousand acres of land to the United States Government. This treaty came just after regular outbreaks of smallpox in the Makah community, to which they lost thousands of tribal members. After the treaty was signed, agents tried to force more laws of assimilation: no potlaches, no ceremonies, no speaking their Native language. The tribe resisted all of these, refusing to let their culture be taken from them.

Once, I was talking about storms and tsunamis with a coworker in Washington, one who had lived a long time and done much good in his life. He clenched his fist in frustration at the Makah's dug-in heels, unwilling to move from their coastal homes. He didn't seem to understand how hard they had fought or how much they had already given up. His voice rose in confused anger as he talked about the members of Makah tribe refusing help and turning away thermal blankets that the well-meaning volunteers offered them.

I nodded along because I understood not only his point but theirs. Relocation feels like the final blow when suggested by a White man, even if it would be safer. History has taught us Natives to be wary of blankets gifted by pale hands. Sometimes they bring death faster than the elements they are meant to shield from. Our numbers cannot weather more devastation than they have already faced since colonizers came. We often choose to risk our lives with nature instead.

⇒.

For days I couldn't get the tribal enrollment numbers out of my head.

542.

297.

Over and over I came back to them. I wanted to twist them into something else, but mostly I just sat in nauseous awe. Unless the laws change, which there is no guarantee of, my tribe will become history in front of me.

I was in the car with a White man I was dating at the time and tried many times to describe the feeling, this vibration that told me something was wrong and something bad was coming even though I was in no immediate danger.

"It's like being at the end of an era," he said, trying to help me navigate the mist in my mind.

"No, not even," I could feel the edge in my voice as I talked. I wasn't angry at him, but I wouldn't let this reality be downplayed into something more comfortable either. "It's literally the end of a people, of my people."

We sat in silence in the parked car. I don't remember where we were or what we were doing, but I remember staring at all of the dials sitting at zero. I felt numb, like the shaking dread had pulled the tide of blood out of me. I spoke as I waited for it to come crashing back with force and overwhelm me in anger and tears.

"It's extinction happening in real time."

# RAVEN'S EMERGENCE

Ravens are problem solvers. They are one of the few creatures capable of seeing a puzzle or obstacle and working their way around it. Oftentimes, they use this skill to obtain food. They have been known to lead wolves to carcasses they can't open themselves or to form tenuous alliances with other unmated ravens to run off a mated pair from a food source. They have been observed using tools to reach morsels of meat, and then recalling those tools later and giving them more value than they do other objects that surround them.

They are tricky, manipulative, cunning corvids and have earned their place as trickster myth in the Pacific Northwest.

≈•

In Western culture, ravens are associated with darkness and death. In Edgar Allan Poe's famous poem "The Raven," the large, black, bird knocking at his door is meant to symbolize the narrator's inevitable death. In Germany and Sweden, they are seen as damned spirits of those who have suffered in life. In Danish folklore, ravens ate hearts, performed other vile acts, and led people astray with their supernatural powers. Across most White beliefs, they are malicious creatures.

These associations have a few roots in reality. First is the night-black plumage of the birds, which in Western culture is often the color that cloaks the villain. Second is their diet, which largely consists of carrion.

Because of their high intelligence, it is rumored that ravens learned that large groups of soldiers marching toward a battlefield was a sign of an upcoming feast, and so they would follow. They became an omen of death only because they were smart enough to understand that death was coming.

In Native culture, specifically the tribes of the Pacific Northwest, Raven is an intelligent trickster, self-serving but still improving the world around them. In some stories, they are the cultural hero, despite this selfishness.

In the original legends, Raven is responsible not only for the sun and moon and stars but also the salmon, creating land, saving people, and providing fire. Even though they are revered as a hero, their heroism is always motivated by selfishness. They deceive and trick, yet still reflect the shadows that are at the core of Western symbolism, just without the malice lacing every move, and often with more positive results.

≫●

I have a darkness in me. Something that shifts beneath the surface of everything I do. This abyss felt oppressive and dangerous for most of my life. It felt like something that would end me if given the chance.

I didn't realize this truth until I took a step back from trying to force myself into different worlds that didn't want me, certain Native communities and White communities. I gave that rustling darkness unpressured space. I moved to New Orleans, a place where fitting in didn't matter as much as it had in every other place I had lived; a city that celebrated life and death and magic and mayhem. I began writing again, this time about my life as a Native woman at the end of a culture. I opened up parts of myself I had long left locked away.

I felt wings unfurl.

I knew that Raven was my totem for some time before this, but I had never connected her to the fluttering night I carried in myself. I thought it was something to be ashamed of, or to deny. When I felt like it would swallow me whole, I would push it back further.

Now I feel that same inky blackness, a storm of feathers, stretch into every part of who I am. I can see her playfulness in every move I make. I can feel her ambition to change the world coursing through me. I think of her teaching Hummingbird to fly and paving the way for the Salish people to move forward. I picture her stealing the sunlight and bringing the world into what it was always meant to be.

Whenever I doubt myself, I remind myself that we are one in spirit. She changed the world and so will I. She is a cultural hero to the Salish people, and I will do my best to be.

She has always been Native enough.

So am I.

# A Note on Sources

The creation of this book would not have been possible without a few key people assisting me. For family stories from before my time, I relied on my mother, Kristy Myers, and my aunt Gloria Smith. Gloria also provided a more in-depth knowledge of the Olympic Peninsula. For tribal history, I must thank my cousin Rachel Sullivan-Owens, the cultural coordinator for the Jamestown S'Klallam Tribe.

For the more widespread research, I made use of several sources in many different essays. Articles and books that were particularly helpful to individual essays are listed here.

## REAL LIVE INDIANS

Discussion of Edward S. Curtis's intentions with his photographic series is informed by Brian W. Dippie's "Photographic Allegories and Indian Destiny," in *Montana: The Magazine of Western History*. Quoted letters and orders from British army officials discussing the use of smallpox in biological warfare come from *Never Come to Peace Again: Pontiac's Uprising and the Fate of the British Empire in North America* by David Dixon (University of Oklahoma Press, 2014).

The history of boarding schools and their effect on Native populations was gathered from Native Partnership's "History and Culture: Boarding Schools" entry, Jeff Gammage's article "Army Begins Unearthing Remains of Children Who Died at Carlisle Indian School" in the *Philadelphia Inquirer*, and the Carlisle Indian School Project.

## AN ANNOTATED GUIDE TO ANTI-NATIVE SLURS

For the history and first recorded implementation of the "Drunken Indian" stereotype, I looked to Tanya Lee's article "Study Says the 'Drunken Indian' Is a Myth" for *Indian Country Today*. For the long history of the slur "redskin," I relied on Ian Shapira's article "A Brief History of the Word 'Redskin' and How it Became a Source of Controversy" in the *Washington Post*.

## SALMON'S MEMORY

I learned much about salmon and their minds and migration instincts while writing this essay. The majority of statistics and facts came from a Seattle Aquarium blog post titled "The How and Why of Salmon Migration."

## A WRITER WHO CAN'T READ

A key source for this essay is obviously the *Klallam Dictionary* by Timothy Montler. I want to thank Professor Montler for working to preserve the language in this tome as well as in his other work, *Klallam Grammar.* I also obtained information from Tim Walker's article about Hazel Sampson, "Last Known Native Speaker of Tribal Klallam Language Hazel Sampson Dies Aged 103," published in the *Independent.*

## HUMMINGBIRD'S MOVEMENT

For the facts and statistics about hummingbirds, I relied on Erica Sánchez Vásquez's article "Ten Fascinating Facts about Hummingbirds," published in the *American Bird Conservancy,* and a study titled "Learning and Spatial Memory in Ruby-Throated Hummingbird (*Archilochus colubris*)" by Samantha Ginsburg et al.

## UNREPORTED VIOLENCE

Sharon Cohen's "#NotInvisible: Why Are Native American Women Vanishing?" story for the *AP News* served as a source for most of the statistics for this essay, and as a pathway to find out updated statistics to reflect more recent numbers. Annita Lucchesi and Abigail Echo-Hawk's *Missing and Murdered Indigenous Women and Girls Report* provided the numbers of missing and murdered Native women in various cities across the country that are quoted in this essay. The final source was a blog post by Sara Vehling titled "Taking Your Breath Away—Why Strangulation in Domestic Violence Is a Huge Red Flag," for its extensive coverage into the dark numbers of strangulation.

## SCALPING KNIFE TURNED SCALPEL

The sources for this essay fall into two groups. The first group contains data on the Indian Child Welfare Act and forced separations and adoptions of Native American children to White families. These were Claire Palmiste's "From the Indian Adoption Project to the Indian Child Welfare Act: The Resistance of Native American Communities" for the *Upstander Project* and Christie Renick's "The Nation's First Family Separation Policy" in *The Imprint*. The second group consists of research and history of the illegal sterilization of Native women. This included *American Indian Quarterly*'s paper from Jane Lawrence titled "The Indian Health Service and the Sterilization of Native American Women" as well as "A 1970 Law Led to the Mass Sterilization of Native

American Women. That History Still Matters" by Brianna Theo-
bald, in *Time*.

## THE SOUND OF THE END

This essay relied on the diligent research of Kathryn Schulz in her
piece "The Really Big One" for the *New Yorker*. The information
about the tsunami that will inevitably hit the northwest, as well
as the effects it will likely have on the area, come from this work.
Other sources for this essay center on infrasound. These are Tim
Radford's article "Silent Sounds Hit Emotional Chords" for *The
Guardian*, Steve Goodman's book *Sonic Warfare: Sound, Affect,
and the Ecology of Fear*, and "The Ghost in the Machine" by Vic
Tandy and Tony Lawrence, in *The Journal of the Society for Psy-
chical Research*.